100 Ways with Cheese

Maggie Black

 Letts**Guides**

Charles Letts and Company Ltd
London, Edinburgh and New York

Acknowledgements
Author and publisher alike owe a marked
debt to many trade organizations and
suppliers who have provided recipes, ideas
and advice generously. Special thanks are
due to Messrs Paxton and Whitfield for
test materials and to Mr A G Smith and
Mrs D Christophers for recipe testing.

The author would also like to give special
thanks to the English Country Cheese
Council, the Farmhouse English Cheese
Division of the Milk Marketing Board, The
Swiss Cheese Union Inc, the Dutch Dairy
Bureau and the Danish Food Centre; also
to Mrs E Sinclair-Thomson of the Flour
Advisory Bureau, Miss Mary Pope and
Miss Patricia Grant, Chief Dietitian,
Charing Cross Hospital, for reviewing
parts of the text.

First published 1976
2nd impression 1976
by Charles Letts and Company Limited
Diary House, Borough Road, London SE1 1DW

Design and illustrations by Ed Perera
Cover photograph by Andrew Thompson

© Maggie Black 1976
ISBN 0 850 97191 8

Printed in Great Britain by
Clarke, Doble and Brendon Limited, Plymouth

Contents

Introduction

Cheese is one of the easiest foods to use. You can eat it either raw or cooked, and it is never boring because there are so many different kinds of cheese. It is suitable for any kind of meal, from a main course for a family, or a big party, to a midday snack for an office worker or a pensioner. You can buy as much or as little as you want at a time; and it is clean, compact, and lightweight to carry home, and easy to store. Most hard or semi-hard cheeses can be stored for a week in any cool place.

Cheese can thus be a boon, especially for disabled or elderly people if they find shopping a problem. It can always be kept in stock as a ready-to-use protein food. It does not take up much space, and does not become unsafe to use by going bad. It does not even lose food value when stored for a while, as most other foods do.

Cheese is one of the easiest foods to eat, too, especially when grated. It then needs less chewing than meat, which makes it especially useful in an elderly person's diet. It is also even easier to cut than bread: it requires a less sharp knife and less heat to cook it.

Cheese is not only easy to handle and eat; it is also very easy to digest if wisely used. Some doctors now recommend it even for babies. If it is grated or eaten in sensible small mouthfuls, or is mixed with other foods and is cooked properly, cheese need never be indigestible.

Choosing and buying cheese

When you choose cheese, the most important thing is to know how you want to use it; in a cooked dish, as a grilled topping, to eat just as it is, or to store as a standby, either in one piece or grated. Both the type and condition of cheese you buy depends on your need. Always buy top grade cheese, no matter what its purpose. A low quality product tastes less attractive, spoils easily in cooking and does not, normally, store well.

Next, try to make sure you get cheese in the right condition for your purpose, whatever type it is. The cheese's age, flavour and texture all contribute to whether it is good value for your needs.

The best way to judge a cheese is to taste it. Even the same type and grade of cheese can vary in flavour a good deal. But of course you cannot taste prewrapped cheeses, or the open cheeses in a store where the staff are busy. Luckily, the way the cheeses are presented and the general surroundings will give you quite a good idea of whether to buy.

No book can tell you all the points to look for, to make sure you get good value when buying cheese. However, here are a few general rules for assessing the condition, age and texture of the main classes of cheeses, both unwrapped and prepackaged.

Hard and semi-hard cheeses: the various types of Cheddar, Cheshire, Lancashire and most other British cheeses come into this class. The cut surface of any of these cheeses is a good guide to its quality. A well-aged Cheddar, for instance, may be slightly flaky, but it should not have cracks in the surface. Nor should it be sweaty or have tiny beads of fat on the cut surface. This often indicates the cheese has been kept uncovered, and too warm for some time.

The colour of the cut surface also gives one some idea of the condition of the cheese. It should be more or less the same colour near the rind and in the centre of the piece. A darker colour near the rind often indicates that the cheese is old and dry; any flecks of white, or a sheen of blue, indicate mould.

If you only want a small amount of cheese, buy a chunk from a small piece of any hard cheese rather than a thin wafer through a whole drum or block. Thin pieces dry out

more quickly and are more difficult to serve or use (eg to grate).

Semi-soft cheeses: the more 'plastic' cheeses such as Edam, Esrom, Port Salut and Gouda come into this category. Usually they are blander and more buttery than the harder cheeses, and should give slightly when pressed with the finger. The cut surface should be velvety, neither moist nor flaky; and the cheese should be the same creamy colour all the way through.

Soft-ripening cheeses: Camembert and Brie are the cheeses we know best in this category, so they are worth describing on their own. They ripen and spoil as quickly as fresh soft cheeses, and they have to be thrown away when overripe because they smell and taste of ammonia. Yet they are tasteless, dry curds if eaten too soon. If you buy a wedge from a wheel with a cut edge, look for a cheese that is glossy all through but not spilling out. A hard cake-like white strip in the centre is unlikely to ripen, if it ripens at all, before the outer cheese goes bad. If you buy a wrapped portion or a whole small uncut Camembert, try to press it lightly with your finger before buying it; it should yield if nearly or quite ready for table. If you cannot touch it, look at it carefully. A soft-ripening cheese should fill its box and not be sunken in the middle.

Soft cheeses: these are of two kinds; real cheeses like a Boursin (and countless other creamy French cheeses) and the fresh, so-called 'cream' cheeses and curd and cottage cheeses. These all become overripe and inedible within a few days, even in a refrigerator, so they should be eaten as soon as possible after you buy them. A soft cheese with a skin or crust should be clean-looking and well shaped, not discoloured or dented; inside, the cheese should be white and even textured, without moisture seeping from it; but it should be soft enough to cut easily with a spoon. Cream, curd and cottage cheeses are much moister, even quite wet.

Blue cheeses: the best known veined blue cheeses are Stilton, Roquefort, Danish Blue and Gorgonzola, but there are many others: the small Bresse Bleu is on sale widely, and you may find Italian Dolcelatte, a French Pipo Creme or an English Blue Wensleydale. Most blue cheeses are fairly pungent, and unpleasantly so when overripe, so they should be bought carefully. Luckily, this is comparatively easy. Any blue cheese should look moist rather than grainy, and it should be creamy right through without discoloured patches. Over-aged blue cheese tends to look greyish and cakey. The type of blue veining may be close-set and dark or paler and more like branching sprays.

But its background should never contain black cracks or dull, dark streaks.

Processed and packaged cheeses: when opened, a processed cheese or cheese spread should be smooth, glossy all over and pliant; normally it will be, because these cheeses are heat-treated to make them last unchanged for some time. If, by some chance, a processed cheese has been spoiled, it will look mouldy and smell sour as soon as it is unwrapped.

Not only processed cheeses but most other cheeses are packaged these days. Even luxury cheeses come in sealed boxes or paper coverings. Other usual kinds of packaging are vacuum packs, foil wraps, and glossy plastic skins, often brightly coloured. So you need some guide to buying wrapped cheeses as a group, to be reasonably sure you are buying as wisely as you can.

There can be no guarantee that a particular cheese is good of its type when you buy it packaged. But here are some points to look for in assessing the quality of a cheese counter or chilled cabinet in any shop; they apply whether it holds packaged or open cheeses:

● Cheeses should be on a separate shelf from other foods and each type of cheese should have its own place, with a gap between it and the type next to it. Strong and mild cheeses should not be next to each other, and certainly not piled up together.

● All cheeses should look good. Even one badly dented or dirty package, or a rusted crust on an open cheese, should make you suspect the rest.

● The cheese's shape should be plump. It should fill out its wrapping, and look and feel smooth, not wrinkled or shrivelled.

Open and examine any packaged cheese as soon as possible after buying it. Take a cheese that is unfit to eat straight back to the retailer if possible. He can return it to his supplier, and should be glad to be told that it has deteriorated. After all, he may have other similar cheeses on his shelves which can contaminate his other goods.

Storing cheese

Any cheese is best stored loosely wrapped in polythene or greaseproof paper. Leave a little air space inside to prevent any sweating or mouldiness. Keep the cheese in a cool place. Remember, however, if you keep it in a refrigerator to take it out at least an hour or two before serving to let the cheese recover its flavour; it will have been dulled by the chilling.

Vacuum-packed cheeses should be kept cooler than unwrapped cheeses. If the surface of the cheese is wet when it is unwrapped, let it dry off naturally before you eat it. If a cheese remains unused for a time and becomes sharp flavoured or begins to go mouldy, it need not be wasted. The only exceptions are the soft cheeses like Camembert which develop an ammonia type smell and must then be thrown away. Any light mould on the harder cheeses can be scraped off, and the cheese can then be used at once or potted (see pp 53–54). If cheese becomes dry with age, simply grate it. Then store it in a screw-topped jar for use in cooking or with salads. This is often the most convenient way to keep it, too, when it is newly bought.

Cheese as a food

Weight for weight cheese contains as much protein as prime raw beef. It has another virtue in that it is one of our richest food sources of calcium which is necessary for healthy teeth and strong bones. It also contains several vitamins. Vitamin A is vital for maintaining good eye-sight in dim light, and it is part of the material which holds the body cells together. Vitamin D, along with calcium, is essential for the development of normal healthy bones. Lack of it can make children deformed. Vitamin B2 (riboflavin) is needed to prevent inflammations such as mouth infections. We find all these vitamins in cheese.

Most cheeses are also rich in fat. A certain amount of fat is essential for keeping warm. So even slimmers should eat some fat, although not too much.

Of course cheese does not supply all the types of food that we require. Our bodies need carbohydrate (from sugars and starches) and other nutrients. Nevertheless, it is easy to make a really well balanced, satisfying meal by adding just a few simple items to a main cheese dish. Bread and butter, cheese and a tomato or orange is just one good combination among many.

How to cook cheese

Cheese must be cooked slowly, over very gentle heat. It should only just melt. Even when cooked with extra fat, it should never spit or burn. The reason for cooking cheese gently is to prevent it becoming rubbery. The solid part of cheese is made up of tiny particles of milk solids surrounded by fat globules. When cheese melts, the particles burst in the heat and mix with the fat. In some cheeses, however, the fat globules melt easily and run off before the solids burst. This means that the cheese, instead of becoming a creamy mixture, turns to a ropey mass of solids with separate globules of fat.

One or two other cooking tips:
● Mature cheese melts and blends more easily with other ingredients than less ripened cheese; and you need less of it because it has a stronger flavour. Farmhouse cheese is thus good for both cooking and eating, although more expensive. Processed cheese also melts easily, but its flavour is usually very mild.

● If you want to cook with one of the cheeses which becomes ropey easily, either grate it, or mix it first with breadcrumbs, flour or a little extra fat. Any of these ingredients will combine with the fat of the cheese itself, absorb some heat when cooking and so prevent the fat running off before the solid particles burst.

● A good way to melt cheese is to put it in a basin which fits over a saucepan of simmering water. Another way is to add it to a hot mixture; for example, add the cheese to a sauce after the sauce has been cooked, or sprinkle it into an omelette just before you fold and serve it.

● If you grill cheese, keep it 4 to 5in from the heat and keep the grill heat low. In a casserole, bake the whole dish at a low temperature. If you use cheese as a topping, grate it and mix it with breadcrumbs before sprinkling it on the dish.

Cheese sauce is used for so many different kinds of dishes that it could be included in any of the following sections. However, since it is also an excellent example of how to cook cheese properly it is shown here as a basic recipe.

Cheese sauce:
thin sauce for soups
1 oz butter
1 oz flour
$1\frac{1}{2}$ pints milk
Seasoning (depending on type of
 cheese)
4–8 oz grated cheese per pint of
 liquid

Melt butter gently, stir in flour, mix well and cook for a few moments without browning. Remove from heat, add milk gradually and blend in. Return to heat, bring to simmering point, stirring continuously, and cook for a few moments until sauce is creamy. Beat well, season. Remove from the heat, stir in cheese a little at a time.

Thicker pouring sauce for mixing with macaroni etc: make as above but only use 1 pint milk.

Coating sauce for covering fish, eggs, meat or vegetables: make as above but only use $\frac{1}{2}$ pint milk.

Thick sauce for souffle base etc: make as above but only use $\frac{1}{4}$ pint milk.

(American: 4, 2, $1\frac{1}{4}$ or $\frac{1}{2}$ and 2 tbsps milk)

Most cheeses are improved by pepper and a very little salt. Some are good with a few grains of Cayenne pepper or a little dry mustard added; or nutmeg can be used as an alternative. Any of these seasonings can be stirred into the sauce or mixed with the cheese. As an alternative, flavour the milk by simmering an onion and a bayleaf in it before use.

Cheese guide

This is a guide to cheeses we buy and eat most often; first British cheeses and then some European ones.

British cheeses

Cheddar is our most famous and widely used cheese. It is copied in many parts of the world, and varies widely in strength of flavour. New Zealand Cheddar, for instance, is usually mild, English Cheddar is of medium strength and most Canadian Cheddar is strong tasting.

English Cheddar is of two main types; Farmhouse and creamery. Farmhouse Cheddar is still made by single families and small dairies. It is of high quality, is matured for a long time, and is more expensive than

9

creamery Cheddar. Creamery Cheddar may be a quickly ripened fairly mild cheese, or be labelled as mature, meaning that it has been allowed to develop for some time before being sold.

All Cheddar should be golden, close in texture, with a clean, nutty flavour. It is first class for eating as it is, especially with fruit, and is an excellent cooking and grating cheese too. It well deserves its fame.

Cheshire can also be a Farmhouse or creamery cheese. It is more salty and acid than Cheddar, and more crumbly. It is naturally white, but a red (dyed) type is widely sold. There is also a blue Cheshire, with broad blue streaks, which is creamy textured but full flavoured like other blue cheeses; to my mind, it is the best of the Blues, not excepting most Stilton.

Any Cheshire makes a good eating cheese, especially with gingerbread or cake, and with apples. It is also a widely used cooking cheese, particularly for traditional English dishes such as toasted cheese or apple pie.

Caerphilly is a mild, white, close textured, slightly salty cheese. It is good with salads and for packed meals and sandwiches, but is not recommended for cooking.

Derby is a honey coloured, open textured cheese, mild when young but tangy when at its best, at about six months old. It is good with biscuits, as a lunch cheese and with fruit. Sage Derby has criss-crossed green lines or a broad band of green running through it, and a flavour of sage leaves.

Double Gloucester is pale orange, open in texture, mild and buttery in flavour. It is good after a solid meat meal, or with beer. It is also a very good, all-purpose cooking cheese. Single Gloucester is no longer made, and some Double Gloucester is now just called Gloucester.

Dunlop and Orkney are Cheddar style cheeses from Scotland. Dunlop is the more mellow; both are slightly softer than Cheddar.

Lancashire is another English cheese which is made both on farms and in creameries. It is the strongest flavoured Farmhouse English cheese, although the creamery cheese is mild. Both are soft, white and crumbly, and excellent for toasted dishes and for crumbling into soups, stews, hot-pots and so on.

Leicester, a rich orange-red cheese, looks and tastes interesting. It is fairly mild but tangy, and makes a good cooking as well as an eating cheese. It may be slightly flaky.

Wensleydale is a white, close textured cheese, not unlike Caerphilly in taste when young; it is mild and slightly salty. On the whole it is better for eating than cooking. Blue Wensleydale is highly reputed. It is less creamy and more salty than blue Cheshire, but has many devotees.

Stilton is beyond doubt the king of English cheeses, if not of all blue cheeses. It is rich, full fat and creamy, best eaten with bread or plain biscuits, and a wonderful accompaniment to wine, especially port. The rind is wrinkled and crusty, and the creamy interior with its dark blue-green veins is itself slightly darker near the crust. Top quality Stilton is made in large drums, although smaller sizes and even jars of ready potted Stilton are available; and it is also widely sold now in film-wrapped wedges. For a party most good cheese merchants will supply half or one-third of a drum split horizontally, so that you can have prime Stilton in a reasonable quantity. It can be used for cooking if left over, or can be potted for storage.

'Cream' cheese may be single cream cheese with a butterfat content of 20 to 25%, or double cream cheese with a butterfat content of 50 to 55%. Single cream cheese keeps for about 4 days in a refrigerator, double cream cheese only 2–3 days. Both are now, strictly, called 'full fat soft' cheeses under the Trade Descriptions Act.

Cottage cheese has a butterfat content of only 4%. It is soft, velvety, and usually granular, and is very moist. It is good in salads and as a dip; but curd cheese makes better cheesecakes.

Curd cheese is a low or medium fat cheese, clean and slightly acid to taste and with a closer texture than cottage cheese. Like all soft cheeses, it must be eaten while fresh.

Other cheeses

Bel Paese is a full fat, ivory coloured Italian cheese. It is mostly used for eating, although it melts easily and is therefore good in cooked dishes and toasted sandwiches.

Brie is one of the most famous French cheeses. It is usually sold in foil-wrapped wedges so you cannot be sure of its quality. It is worth visiting a speciality shop which sells Brie from a whole 14-inch cartwheel cheese, since Brie must be eaten when in peak condition (see p 5).

Camembert is France's most plentiful cheese. We usually buy it wrapped, either in a whole round, half round or in small wedges, and, again, you have to take a chance on its quality, since it is usually kept very cool in a store and is firmer than it will be at room temperature (see p 5).

Danish Blue cheese is of two types, and the slightly milder, more yellowish **Mycella** is worth looking for, although it is rarer. It is more aromatic and subtle. Both cheeses are rich in fat, and can be used for either eating or cooking.

Edam is normally a skimmed milk cheese. It has a bright red rind, and should give a little when pressed. Its flavour is smooth and bland. It is not a good cooking cheese, but it is excellent for everyday eating (especially for slimmers). It tastes best if each helping is peeled in thin slices from the whole piece, either with a sharp knife or cheese slicer.

Esrom, Samsoe and **Havarti** are all good Danish cheeses, mild in flavour but firmer in texture than Edam. Esrom and Havarti have holes in them, rather like Gruyere. They are generally used as table cheeses.

Emmentaler is Swiss by origin, and the best quality cheeses still come from Switzerland. Emmentaler is made from very high quality milk; its curd is yellow-ivory with large holes in it. It is famous as a cooking cheese, and is often used mixed with Parmesan. It is also the cheese most used for a classic Swiss cheese fondue.

Gorgonzola is a well known Italian blue cheese, rich, creamy and pungent. Its veins are pale green rather than blue. Its younger brother, **Dolcelatte**, is milder. Both are mainly used for eating.

Gouda is a Dutch semi-soft cheese, a good full fat relation of Edam, although with a yellow rind. It is bland when young, but sharpens pleasantly in flavour as it matures. It is good with brown bread and in sandwiches, but also makes a good, easy-to-use cooking cheese.

Gruyere is another Swiss born cheese, although it is now widely made elsewhere because it is so popular. The curd is yellow-ivory and firm, even hard when it ages, and it has small irregular holes scattered throughout. It is excellent cooking cheese.

Parmesan is the most famous Italian cheese, especially for cooking. We usually get it when two to three years old, when it is mature, hard and very pungent; so we often use it mixed with another cheese such as Gruyere or Emmentaler. Most Parmesan is now sold ready grated in small drums or cartons. But the flavour is, of course, fresher if it is bought in the piece and is grated at home.

Roquefort is easily the best known French blue cheese, famous for its strong, rich flavour. Imported Roquefort may be very salty. If a piece proves too salty for the table, it can be used in salads, as a salad dressing (see p 31), and in certain cooked dishes. But it is mainly known as a table cheese.

12

Weights and measures

All ingredient quantities are given in British Standard measurements, and the appropriate American measures for each ingredient follow at the foot of every recipe. Note that American spoon measures are smaller than British spoons:

1 British teaspoon equals $1\frac{1}{4}$ American teaspoons
1 British tablespoon equals $1\frac{1}{4}$ American tablespoons

The following metric equivalents apply for measuring ingredients, but note that metric measures are always given as convenient round figures and are only approximate equivalents. When converting large quantities one obtains slightly less of the finished product than when using ounces and pounds.

1 oz is taken as 25gm
4 oz are taken as 100gm
8 oz are taken as 200gm
1 lb is taken as 500gm

1 teaspoon is taken as 5ml
  (American teasp 4·8ml)
1 tablespoon is taken as 15ml
  (American tbsp 14·8ml)
$\frac{1}{4}$ pint is taken as 125ml
1 pint is taken as 500ml
2 pints are taken as 1 litre

Equivalent oven temperatures

250°F	Mark $\frac{1}{2}$	130°C
275°F	Mark 1	140°C
300°F	Mark 2	145°C
325°F	Mark 3	160°C
350°F	Mark 4	175°C
375°F	Mark 5	190°C
400°F	Mark 6	200°C
425°F	Mark 7	220°C
450°F	Mark 8	230°C

Abbreviations

teasp—teaspoon
tbsp—tablespoon
dessertsp—dessertspoon

In these recipes Philadelphia cream cheese spread is called rich full fat soft cheese.

Cheese starters and soups

Here are a few light dishes and soups to start a meal. You will find others on pp 29–30. Give to guests, or to a hungry family, while you dish up the main course.

Stuffed tomato starters

Serves 4
4 medium tomatoes, skinned
¼ cucumber, diced
salt
2 × 3 oz pkts rich full-fat soft cheese
1 dessertsp single cream
1 tbsp chopped chives
pinch of Cayenne pepper
4 × 2 inch rounds brown bread
butter for spreading
2 tbsps olive oil
1 tbsp mild white vinegar
salt and pepper
pinch of sugar
chopped parsley
watercress
walnut halves

Cut tops off tomatoes and scoop out flesh. Sieve inside flesh, keep aside. Turn tomato shells upside down to drain. Sprinkle cucumber with salt, leave 30 minutes. Rinse and dry. Mix cucumber with cheese, cream, chives and Cayenne. Mix well then spoon filling into tomatoes. Replace tops. Place each tomato on a buttered bread round. Mix oil, vinegar, seasoning and tomato pulp. Spoon over tomatoes. Decorate with parsley, watercress and walnuts. Serve one per person.

(American: 1 tbsp light cream, 3 tbsps oil, 1½ tbsps vinegar, 1½ tbsps parsley)

Stuffed eggs

Serves 4
4 eggs
2 oz butter
2 oz full-fat soft cheese
1 tbsp milk
1 stick celery, chopped
salt and Cayenne pepper
lettuce leaves
mayonnaise

Boil eggs 10 minutes, shell and cool. Cut in half lengthways. Remove yolks without breaking whites. Cream the butter, and blend in the cheese, yolks, milk and celery. Season to taste. Pile mixture into egg whites. Lay whites on lettuce leaves, and top each with a spoonful of mayonnaise.
(American: 1¼ tbsps milk)

Mock crab

Serves 4
1 hard-boiled egg yolk
1 tbsp salad oil
½ teasp onion salt
½ teasp caster sugar
¼ tbsp made English mustard
1 tbsp mild white vinegar
4 oz red Leicester cheese, shredded
1 tbsp chicken or tuna, shredded

For decoration:
2 radishes thinly sliced
lettuce leaves
thin brown bread and butter

Use Cheddar and 1 teasp tomato purée if you cannot get Leicester. Sieve egg yolk. Mash most of it to a smooth paste with the oil, using the back of a spoon. Reserve remaining yolk. Mix the paste with seasonings and vinegar until smooth. In a separate bowl, mix cheese and chicken or tuna lightly with a fork, keeping shreds separate. Mix lightly with other ingredients and chill. To serve, lay in piles on lettuce leaves and decorate with lines of overlapping radish slices. Sprinkle reserved yolk over. Cut crusts off bread, roll up, and serve 2 rolls with each helping.

Clear soup with eggs

Serves 4
4 eggs
2 × 15 oz cans beef consomme
4 rounds white bread, toasted
4 oz Cheddar cheese, finely grated

Poach eggs lightly in consomme or in greased cups in an egg poacher. Heat soup, and warm 4 soup bowls. Place a round of toast in each bowl, and place eggs on top. Pour consomme over, sprinkle well with the cheese and serve at once while hot. Alternatively, serve:

Cheese croutons (for soup garnish):
Cut crusts off 2 slices white bread. Toast lightly one side only. Mix 1 oz cheese, 1 tbsp beaten egg yolk and 2 teasps melted butter, and spread all over untoasted bread. Bake or grill gently until bubbling. Cool slightly. Cut into cubes. Hand with soup.

(American: $1\frac{1}{2}$ tbsps eggs, $2\frac{1}{2}$ teasps butter)

Cheddar and vegetable soup

Serves 2–3
4–5 oz carrot (2 medium)
4–5 oz turnip (1 medium)
2–3 oz celery (1–2 sticks)
1–$1\frac{1}{2}$ oz onion (1 small)
$\frac{3}{4}$ pint chicken or vegetable stock
1 heaped tbsp flour
$\frac{1}{4}$ pint warm milk
3–4 oz Cheddar cheese
salt and pepper
pinch of sugar

Scrape or skin vegetables and shred them. Simmer in $\frac{1}{2}$ pint stock for 10–15 minutes until tender. Mix flour to a paste with a little of remaining stock, stir into vegetables. Add remaining stock and simmer 2–3 minutes. Grate cheese and add with milk, seasoning and sugar. Serve quickly.

(American: 2 cups stock, 2 tbsps flour and a generous $\frac{1}{2}$ cup milk)

Potato soup

Serves 4
1 lb potatoes

1 medium onion
1 small green pepper
1 oz margarine
1½ pints chicken stock (from cube)
    or vegetable water
1 × 3 oz pkt rich full-fat soft cheese
3 tbsps milk
chopped parsley

Peel potatoes and slice thickly. Skin onion and pepper and chop finely. Melt margarine in a saucepan, add onion and pepper and cook gently without colouring until soft. Add potatoes, pour on stock, heat and simmer for 45 minutes, covered. Sieve soup and return to saucepan. Blend milk into cheese, sieve into soup. Reheat until almost boiling, and serve topped with parsley.

(American: 4 tbsps milk)

Pears with Stilton

4 helpings
2 hard cooking pears
juice 1 lemon
4 oz blue Stilton cheese, thinly sliced
fat for greasing

Peel pears, halve, dig out any hard core with a small spoon. Cut in thin slices lengthways. Simmer in water and lemon juice with small pinch of salt. Remove while still firm in centre but softened at edges. Drain. Grease a flat flameproof plate. Lay pear slices side by side or in a circle with narrow ends inward. Cover with cheese slices, trimming off overhanging bits. Crumble trimmings on top. Grill under low heat until cheese bubbles and browns. Serve at once with pumpernickel or dark rye bread.

Cheese with meat and fish

Cheese can be a boon if you want to make an economical yet nourishing dish or to use up leftovers; it supplements the protein value of small amounts of meat or fish quickly and easily. Likewise, it adds flavour to white meat or fish which need it. A golden cheese crust or sauce makes any dish look good too.

Tangy steaks

Serves 4
4 rump steaks, about 6 oz each
Worcester sauce to taste
salt and freshly ground black pepper
French mustard
oil for grilling
8 thin slices tomato or green pepper
3–4 oz Cheddar cheese, sliced
watercress sprigs

Beat steaks to flatten slightly.
Sprinkle with sauce and seasoning
on both sides, and spread lightly
with mustard. Allow to stand for
$\frac{1}{2}$–1 hour. Heat grill with grilling
rack or plate in place below. Brush
steaks with oil. Place on heated rack
or plate and grill both sides as
desired. Remove from heat, top with
tomato or pepper slices, then with
sliced cheese. Lower grill heat, then
return steaks and let cheese melt.
Serve at once, garnished with
watercress.

Spicy shepherds pie

Serves 4–6
$1\frac{1}{4}$ lb lean beef mince
2 medium onions
1 oz dripping
1 tbsp flour
$\frac{1}{2}$ tbsp curry powder
6 fl oz beef stock
salt and black pepper
1 tbsp mango chutney
$1\frac{1}{2}$ lb potatoes

butter
3 oz grated Gouda cheese

Break up any lumps in meat. Skin
and slice onions and fry in dripping
until soft. Mix flour and curry
powder, stir into pan and cook 1–2
minutes. Add stock gradually,
stirring. Heat to the boil, and
simmer until sauce thickens. Stir in
meat, cover and simmer 20 minutes.
Mix in seasoning and chutney, and
continue cooking about 10 minutes
or until meat is tender.

While meat cooks, boil potatoes,
skin and mash with more seasoning
and a little butter. Mix in cheese.
Place cooked meat and sauce in a
lightly buttered ovenproof dish,
cover with cheesy potato and bake
10–15 minutes at 425°F, Gas 7, until
brown on top. Serve with sprouts
mixed with diced Gouda and butter.

(American: $1\frac{1}{4}$ tbsps each flour and
chutney, good $\frac{1}{2}$ tbsp curry powder,
$\frac{3}{4}$ cup stock)

Cheesy oven-fried chops

Serves 4
unsalted butter and oil as needed
   (see recipe)
4 large lamb chops
breadcrumbs and egg for coating
pinch each dried parsley and thyme
pinch of grated lemon peel
1 tbsp grated mild cheese
2 oz grated cheese for topping

parsley sprigs
cucumber salad

Heat oven to 350°F, Gas 4. Place butter and oil in pan for cooking chops, using enough to coat base well. Place dish in the oven. Mix breadcrumbs with flavouring and 1 tbsp cheese. Brush chops with egg, then coat with cheese crumb mixture, pressing it on firmly. Remove hot dish from oven and place chops in it, in one layer. Return to oven, bake uncovered for about 20 minutes. Turn chops over, bake a further 10–20 minutes until fully cooked and browned on both sides. Top each chop with $\frac{1}{2}$ oz grated cheese and raise heat to 375°F, Gas 5, for the last 5–6 minutes cooking time. Serve topped with parsley and with cucumber salad as side dish.

(American: $1\frac{1}{2}$ tbsps cheese)

Pressed brisket kebabs

Serves 2
4 oz cooked pressed brisket
2 oz Gouda cheese
2 oz onion, thickly sliced
2 oz mushrooms
oil for brushing kebabs

Cut brisket and cheese into $\frac{1}{2}$ inch cubes. Separate onion layers. Quarter mushrooms. Thread the items alternately on 4 skewers. Brush with oil, and grill under high heat,

20

turning frequently until brown. Serve with salad.

Gammon and banana steaks

Serves 4
4 thin gammon steaks
pepper as needed
4 bananas, peeled
2 oz grated Swiss Emmentaler cheese

Trim rind from steaks. Season with pepper, roll each steak round a banana, and pack closely in an ovenproof dish. Sprinkle well with cheese. Bake at 375°F, Gas 5, for 30–40 minutes.

Ham olives

Serves 4
6 tbsps dry sage and onion stuffing
   (from packet)
12 tbsps boiling water
3 oz slice Gouda cheese at least
   $\frac{1}{2}$ inch thick
2 eggs, beaten
4 large square slices cooked shoulder
   ham, about 1 oz each
4 tbsps thick tomato sauce or
   condensed tomato soup
2 oz finely grated Gouda cheese
beef stock as needed (from cube if
   desired)

Make up the stuffing with water as directed. Leave to stand 30 minutes. Cut cheese slice into 4 fingers. Mix stuffing with eggs. Place 1 tbsp stuffing in a finger shape in centre of each ham slice. Lay cheese finger on stuffing. Cover with more stuffing, and spoon surrounding stuffing over to cover cheese completely. Roll up ham slices and place side by side with cut edges underneath in a shallow ovenproof baking dish. Top each ham roll with 1 tbsp tomato sauce or soup, and sprinkle with $\frac{1}{2}$ oz grated cheese. Pour enough stock into the dish to come half-way up the rolls. Bake at 350°F, Gas 4, for 15–20 minutes until stuffing is firm and cheese topping golden. Serve hot with baked jacket potatoes and a green salad.

(American: 7$\frac{1}{2}$ tbsps stuffing, 15 tbsps water, 6 tbsps sauce or soup)

Chicken or turkey divan

Serves 4
4 heads frozen broccoli, thawed
salt and pepper
2 dessertsps melted butter
3 dessertsps grated Parmesan cheese
6 dessertsps dry sherry
4 thick slices cooked chicken or
 turkey breast
1 egg yolk
8 fl oz white sauce (from packet if
 desired)
1 dessertsp double cream (optional)

Simmer broccoli in a little lightly salted water until tender. Drain well and season. Brush a shallow ovenproof dish with a little of the butter. Lay in the broccoli. Sprinkle with the remaining butter,

1 dessertsp cheese and 2 dessertsps sherry. Place chicken or turkey in 1 layer on top. Sprinkle with second dessertsp cheese and 2 dessertsps sherry. Blend egg yolk into sauce. Stir in cream if used. Heat very gently, stirring continuously. When hot and creamy, pour sauce over meat. Sprinkle with remaining cheese and pour sherry over. Bake at 350°F, Gas 4, for 15–20 minutes.

(American: 2 tbsps butter, 3 tbsps cheese, 6 tbsps sherry, 1 cup sauce, 1 tbsp heavy cream)

Salami appleburgers

Serves 4
4 soft round bread rolls or baps
2 oz unsalted butter
4 thick slices salami or luncheon
 meat roll
4 thick round slices cored apple
salt, pepper and pinch of ground
 mace or cloves
4 slices processed cheese
$\frac{1}{4}$ pint coating cheese sauce (see p 9)

Split rolls, toast cut sides lightly. Butter. Cover bottom halves with meat, top with apple, season. Cover apple with cheese and trim slice to cover toasted bread but not overhang. Divide remaining butter into 4 knobs, place 1 on each cheese slice. Grill briefly until cheese begins to melt. Replace tops of rolls

21

or baps, cover with heated cheese sauce, and serve at once. Good with tomato salad.

(American: generous $\frac{1}{2}$ cup cheese sauce)

Golden guinea cod

Serves 2
2 × 4 oz frozen cod steaks
salt to taste
$\frac{1}{4}$ pint rich milk
$2\frac{1}{2}$ oz Gouda cheese
2 eggs
pepper to taste
Cayenne pepper to taste
grated nutmeg to taste
2 tomatoes or 1 cooked courgette
butter as needed

Cut cod steaks into 3 fingers each lengthways. Poach gently in slightly salted milk for 5–7 minutes until thawed and cooked through. Grate cheese. Mix 2 oz cheese with eggs, beat well. Put cheese and egg mixture in a small saucepan. Drain hot milk from cooking fish on to mixture, stirring continuously. Season to taste. Heat gradually, still stirring, until sauce thickens. Place fish on a flameproof plate or dish, and strain sauce over. Cut tomatoes in half horizontally, courgette lengthways. Season and sprinkle remaining cheese and dabs of butter on cut sides. Place fish and tomatoes or courgette, buttered side up, on

grill rack. Grill 4–5 minutes until cheese is lightly brown. Serve at once.

(American: generous $\frac{1}{2}$ cup milk)

Fish and macaroni pie

Serves 4
1 lb hake or fresh haddock
salt and pepper
$\frac{1}{4}$ pint milk
1 oz butter
8–10 oz quick cooking macaroni
$\frac{1}{2}$ pint coating cheese sauce, heated (see p 9)
butter for greasing
$1\frac{1}{2}$ oz grated Cheddar cheese
melted butter as needed
parsley sprig

Place fish in a saucepan, season and pour in milk. Shred and add butter, and simmer for 8–10 minutes until fish flakes easily. Cook macaroni according to directions while fish cooks. Drain fish well and flake it. Drain macaroni. Add fish and macaroni to cheese sauce. Season.

Grease a flameproof dish and turn in the fish and macaroni mixture. Sprinkle with the grated cheese and enough melted butter to moisten it lightly. Either place in the oven at high heat for a few moments or place under a gentle grill, to brown the cheese topping. Garnish with the parsley just before serving.

(American: $\frac{1}{2}$ cup + 2 tbsps milk, $1\frac{1}{4}$ cups cheese sauce)

Creamy coley bake

Serves 3–4
2 × 6 oz frozen coley fillets
4 fl oz water
few drops lemon juice
1 dessertsp tomato puree
bay leaf
a few parsley stalks
1 × 8 oz pkt broccoli spears
salt and pepper
3 dessertsps melted butter
4 dessertsps grated Gouda cheese
4 dessertsps stock in which coley
   cooked (see recipe)
8 fl oz rich milk
2 egg yolks

Separate fillets. Mix water with juice and puree. Place in shallow pan, add fillets, bay leaf and parsley. Simmer fish until tender. Meanwhile simmer broccoli in a little salted water until tender. Drain both, season and reserve liquid (stock). Brush a shallow ovenproof dish with a little butter. Lay broccoli in the dish, sprinkle with 1 dessertsp butter, 2 dessertsps cheese and 2 dessertsps stock. Lay fillets in one layer on top, sprinkle with 1 dessertsp cheese and 2 of stock. Blend milk and egg yolks, and heat very gently, stirring continuously, until sauce thickens. Season and pour over fish. Top with remaining cheese, sprinkle with butter. Bake at 350°F, Gas 4, for 15–20 minutes.

(American: 1 tbsp puree, 3 tbsps butter, 4 tbsps each cheese and stock)

Smoked cod and noodles

Serves 4
4 oz ribbon noodles
1 lb smoked cod or haddock fillet
$1\frac{1}{2}$ oz margarine
1 oz flour
$\frac{3}{4}$ pint milk
salt and pepper to taste
pinch of paprika
2 oz Parmesan and 1 oz Gruyere
   cheese, grated and mixed

Cook noodles in boiling, salted water as directed on packet. Drain and keep hot. Poach fish in unsalted water for 5–8 minutes. Drain. Remove bones and skin, and flake. Melt 1 oz margarine, mix in flour and cook for a few minutes without colouring. Add milk gradually, stirring continuously. Bring gently to boil, simmer 2–3 minutes. Season well. Grease an ovenproof casserole or dish, and place alternate layers of noodles and fish in it. Pour sauce over, and sprinkle with the cheese. Dot with remaining butter. Reheat in oven at 350°F, Gas 4, for 10–15 minutes or until surface is lightly browned.

(American: 2 cups milk)

Meatless cheese meals

In this section you will find recipes for cheese with pasta, rice and vegetables, as salads and in dressings.

Pasta or vegetables make a satisfying meal without meat or fish, provided their protein content is high enough. Cheese is an excellent food to use for adding extra protein, being both concentrated and flavoursome. For instance, you only need a little cheese to make a nourishing, well flavoured sauce or topping.

Macaroni cheese

Serves 2–3
4 oz quick cooking macaroni
1½ oz flour
¾ pint milk
2 oz margarine
salt and pepper to taste
4 heaped tbsps grated Cheddar
    cheese
a few grains Cayenne pepper
browned breadcrumbs or extra
    grated cheese

Cook macaroni as directed on packet. While cooking, put flour in a bowl and mix to a paste with a little of the milk. Bring remaining milk and margarine to the boil in a pan, pour gradually on to flour paste, stirring. Return whole mixture to pan, and heat gently, still stirring, until sauce thickens. Season, add cheese and Cayenne, stir until melted. Drain macaroni well, pile on warmed dish, coat with sauce and top with crumbs or extra cheese. Brown top under grill if desired.

(American: 2 cups milk, 5 tbsps cheese)

Special creamy spaghetti

Serves 4
12 oz spaghetti
2 oz butter
4 oz sliced mushrooms
1 green pepper, seeded and chopped
1 oz flour
2 teasps dry English mustard
6 fl oz milk
¼ pint single cream
salt and pepper
3 oz grated Cheddar cheese

Cook spaghetti in boiling salted water until tender. Melt 1 oz butter in a saucepan, stir in vegetables. Cook 4–5 minutes, then stir in flour and mustard. Remove from heat, mix in milk gradually. Return to heat, bring to boil slowly, stirring continuously. Lower heat and simmer gently 4–5 minutes, still stirring. Add cream and season. Stir in 2 oz cheese. Drain cooked spaghetti, and toss with remaining butter in dry pan. Transfer to serving dish, cover with sauce. Sprinkle with remaining cheese.

(American: ¾ cup milk, generous ½ cup light cream)

Savoury rice or risotto

Serves 4
1 small onion
2 oz margarine
12 oz uncooked long grain rice
1 teasp condensed tomato puree
2 pints vegetable stock or water
    from boiled vegetables
2 oz grated Cheddar cheese
salt and pepper to taste

Skin and chop onion. In a large pan, fry onion in 1 oz fat until soft. Add rice and puree, and stir until coated with fat. Add warm liquid gradually, letting rice absorb each addition before adding more. Cook gently until all liquid is absorbed and rice is tender. Stir in remaining fat, cheese and seasoning. Serve at once.

Variations:

1. Add a pinch of grated nutmeg and 1 teasp finely chopped parsley with seasoning.

2. Add 1–2 tbsps seedless raisins, soaked beforehand, with seasonings, and a few blanched flaked almonds if liked.

3. Add $\frac{1}{2}$ a finely chopped green pepper, 1 small, skinned, chopped tomato and 1 teasp dried basil with seasoning.

4. Add 1–2 tbsps cooked peas, 1 tbsp chopped cooked mushrooms and 1 teasp dried thyme or marjoram with seasoning.

(American: 5 cups liquid; *variations*: extra puree, peas, mushrooms and herbs as desired)

Potato gratin

Serves 4
2 lb potatoes
butter
12 oz Swiss Gruyere cheese
2 eggs
1 pint milk
pinch each salt and grated nutmeg
salad

Wash and peel potatoes. Slice into $\frac{1}{2}$-inch rounds. Butter a shallow ovenproof serving dish. Slice cheese thinly. Place alternate layers of potatoes and cheese in the dish until $\frac{2}{3}$ full. Beat eggs into milk and season well. Pour mixture over potatoes and cheese. Dot with flakes of butter, and bake at 350°F, Gas 4, for 40–50 minutes until potatoes are brown and tender. Serve with salad.

(American: $2\frac{1}{2}$ cups milk)

Potato croquettes

Serves 4 as main dish with sauce
Serves 6 as side dish without sauce
1 lb cooked potatoes
1 oz butter
2 egg yolks or 1 whole egg
salt and pepper to taste
pinch of ground mace
2 tbsps dry grated Cheddar cheese
extra egg yolk as needed
fine dry breadcrumbs as needed
fat or oil for deep frying
apple-cheese sauce, if main dish

Sieve or mash potatoes, mix well with butter, egg, seasoning and cheese. Form into small rolls. Coat well with extra egg and roll in crumbs. Fry at about 380°F for 4–5 minutes until golden all over. Drain well and serve, with heated sauce if used.

(American: $2\frac{1}{2}$–3 tbsps cheese)

26

Apple-cheese sauce

(for cauliflower, celery and other vegetables)

Serves 4
1 oz butter
1 oz flour
$\frac{1}{2}$ pint milk
$1 \times 4\frac{1}{2}$ oz can strained apple baby
   food
4 oz grated Gouda cheese
salt and pepper to taste
pinch of Cayenne pepper or grated
   nutmeg

Make thick white sauce with butter, flour and milk. Add strained apple food and cheese. Season, heat and use as desired.

This sauce is also good over sausages, hamburgers, etc.

(American: $1\frac{1}{4}$ cups milk)

Cheese and onion batter

Serves 4
2 oz butter
3 medium onions
2 oz grated mild Cheddar cheese
salt to taste
pinch of dry English mustard
4 oz flour
1 egg
$\frac{1}{2}$ pint milk

Use 1 oz butter to grease a pie dish. Skin onions and slice thinly. Lay in the pie dish, sprinkle with cheese mixed with seasonings. Dot with remaining butter. Sift flour into a bowl with a pinch of salt. Beat egg until liquid. Make a well in the flour, pour in egg and add milk gradually, beating continuously, to make a smooth batter. Pour over the cheese and onions. Bake at 375°F, Gas 5, for 45–50 minutes until batter is well risen and onions are tender when skewered.

(American: $1\frac{1}{4}$ cups milk)

Cheese and vegetable pie

Serves 2–3
4 medium potatoes
2 medium onions
1 medium carrot, grated
good $\frac{1}{4}$ pint coating cheese sauce
   (see p 9)
salt, pepper and nutmeg
1 oz grated Cheddar cheese

Peel potatoes and slice thinly. Skin onions and slice into thin rings. Grease an ovenproof casserole, and layer potatoes, carrot and onions in it, seasoning to taste. Make cheese sauce and pour over vegetables. Season the extra grated cheese to taste and sprinkle over sauce. Bake at 375°F, Gas 5, for about 45 minutes, until vegetables are tender when skewered.

(American: $\frac{3}{4}$ cup sauce)

Spinach and cheese cutlets

Serves 4–5
2 × 8 oz pkts frozen chopped spinach
½ oz margarine
8 oz grated Cheddar cheese
salt and pepper
good pinch of nutmeg
2 egg yolks, beaten
extra egg yolk and breadcrumbs for
    coating
butter for frying

Cook spinach as directed. Stir over
heat until water has evaporated.
Stir in margarine and cool. Mix in
cheese and seasonings, and beat in
2 egg yolks. Chill well to firm up,
then form into 8–10 oval patties.
Coat twice firmly with egg yolk and
crumbs. Fry in butter until golden
brown on each side, or grill dry
under moderate heat, turning once.

Cauliflower cheese

Serves 2–3
1 small cauliflower
good ¼ pint coating cheese sauce
    (see p 9)
½ oz grated Cheddar cheese
½ oz browned or fried breadcrumbs

Cook cauliflower, covered, in a
little salted boiling water until just
tender. Drain well and place in
buttered flameproof serving dish.
Keep warm. Make sauce and coat
cauliflower. Mix grated cheese and
crumbs, sprinkle over sauce. Place

dish under gentle grill or in hot oven
for 2–3 minutes to soften topping.

Variation: Cook shredded cabbage
and treat like cauliflower.

(American: ¾ cup sauce)

Broccoli and creamed egg supper

For each person use:
2 oz fresh or frozen broccoli
    (2–3 heads)
pinch of grated nutmeg
salt and pepper
1 × 6 inch long soft roll or piece of
    French bread
1 egg
1 tbsp double cream or skim milk
    powder
3–4 tbsps stock or water from
    cooking broccoli
butter as needed
2 dessertsps grated Parmesan cheese

Trim stems off broccoli, season and
steam over simmering water until
tender. Split roll horizontally and
toast cut sides lightly. Mix egg with
seasoning, cream or milk powder
and stock. Melt butter in a pan and
scramble egg to consistency desired.
Butter the toasted bread. Arrange
broccoli on one half in an attractive
pattern with heads showing over
1 long side. Pile egg on second half.
Top both with cheese. Sprinkle with
butter. Place briefly under gentle
grill until topping softens. To serve,

place bread halves side by side with broccoli heads outward, and half close like semi-split roll. A decorative, novel toasted sandwich.

(American: 1¼ tbsps cream or milk powder, 4–5 tbsps stock or water, 2 tbsps cheese)

Egg and celery bake

Serves 4
4 eggs
½ pint cheese sauce (see p 9), or
    1 pkt cheese sauce mix and
    ½ pint milk
1 × 14 oz can celery hearts in water
salt and pepper
1 oz mild Cheddar cheese
1 oz dried breadcrumbs or ready-
    to-use crumbs from packet

Hard-boil the eggs. Make sauce or make up sauce mix as directed. Drain celery, cut into chunks and pack into bottom of a well greased shallow oven-to-table baking dish. Season. Slice eggs and arrange on celery. Pour sauce over both. Lastly, grate cheese, mix with crumbs and sprinkle over the dish. Bake at 375°F, Gas 5, for 25–30 minutes.

(American: 1¼ cups sauce or milk)

Cheese and cucumber salad

Serves 4
8 oz diced Cheddar cheese
8 oz diced unpeeled cucumber
3 teasps lemon juice
pinch each dry mustard and Cayenne
    pepper
lettuce leaves
4 quartered, skinned tomatoes
brown bread and butter

Toss cheese and cucumber, juice and seasonings. Make a bed of lettuce leaves, arrange cheese mixture on top with tomatoes round. Serve with bread and butter.

(American: extra lemon juice to taste)

Cabbage, cheese and raisin slaw

Serves 4–6
8 oz finely shredded white cabbage
8 oz grated Cheddar cheese
2 oz seedless raisins
3–4 tbsps mayonnaise
1 level teasp salt
pinch of Cayenne pepper

Toss all ingredients lightly together. Chill before serving. Good with cold beef or lamb.

(American: 4–5 tbsps mayonnaise, extra salt if desired)

Tomato and celery salad

Serves 4
4 medium tomatoes, skinned
4 sticks celery
8 oz finely diced Cheddar cheese

4 tbsps salad cream
lettuce leaves
1 oz chopped nuts
1 teasp grated orange peel

Cut tomatoes into small pieces, chop celery, mix with cheese. Pour salad cream over, and fork in lightly. Make a bed of lettuce leaves, and pile mixture on top. Scatter nuts and grated peel over.

(American: 5 tbsps salad cream and $\frac{1}{4}$ teasp extra grated peel)

Fruit and yogurt lunch salad

Serves 3–4 as main course
Serves 6–8 as side dish
8 oz grapes
4 red apples
juice of 1 lemon
8 oz Wensleydale cheese
8 fl oz natural yogurt
lettuce leaves

Halve and pip grapes. Core apples without peeling, cut in $\frac{1}{2}$ inch cubes, toss in lemon juice. Cut cheese in $\frac{1}{2}$ inch cubes. Toss grapes, apples and cheese lightly in yogurt, taking care not to break cheese cubes. Pile on lettuce leaves.

(American: 1 cup yogurt)

Apple and walnut salad

Serves 4
1 lb red skinned dessert apples
12 oz grated Cheddar cheese

1 level teasp celery salt
4 tbsps salad cream
lettuce leaves
2 oz chopped walnuts
watercress as needed

Core, quarter and dice apples. Toss cheese with salt, mix with apples and salad cream. Make a bed of lettuce leaves, pile apple and cheese mixture on top. Sprinkle with nuts. Decorate with watercress.

(American: extra salt if needed, and 5 tbsps salad cream)

Harlequin salad

Serves 4
3 oz Cheshire cheese
3 oz red Leicester cheese
3 oz blue Stilton cheese
3 oz Wensleydale cheese
1 lettuce
4 tomatoes
$\frac{1}{2}$ cucumber
1 tbsp chopped chives
1 small bunch watercress
4 fl oz soured cream
milk if needed

Cut the cheeses into small cubes and jumble together without breaking. Wash and dry lettuce, slice tomato and cucumber, pick over chives and chop cress. Place lettuce and cress on a flat oval platter. Pile cheeses in centre. Mix cream with milk if needed, to obtain a thick pouring consistency. Pour round the cheeses, drip a little over them. Decorate rim of platter with tomato and cucumber and sprinkle whole dish with chives.

(American: 1½ tbsps chives)

Cheddar dressing

4 fl oz olive oil
¼ teasp salt
pinch of freshly ground black pepper
2–3 tbsps mild vinegar
2 dessertsps finely grated Cheddar
  cheese (not too hard)

Mix all ingredients in a screw top jar. Close tightly, and shake vigorously to blend. Adjust seasoning. Chill until needed. Good with any green salad.

Variation: add pinch of sugar and use onion salt.

(American: ½ teasp salt, 3 tbsps vinegar, 2 tbsps cheese)

Blue cheese cream dressing

8 fl oz soured cream
2 spring onion bulbs, finely chopped
2 tbsps lemon juice
3oz any blue cheese, crumbled
salt and pepper to taste

Blend all ingredients, and leave for several hours before using. Good with cucumber or white cabbage salad.

(American: 1 cup cream, 2½ tbsps juice)

Cheesecakes and other cheese desserts

We do not often think of using cheese for sweet dishes. But it can be delicious; and it makes nourishing desserts, much better for the diet-conscious than starchy, sugary puddings.

Cheddar cheesecake

Serves 6–8
1 8 inch pastry flan case or shell,
   baked 'blind'
6 oz grated Cheddar cheese
1 egg yolk
$2\frac{1}{2}$ fl oz natural yogurt
peel and juice of 1 lemon
1 oz self-raising flour
3 oz caster sugar
2 egg whites

Mix cheese, egg yolk, yogurt, grated peel and strained juice of lemon, flour and sugar. Whisk egg whites until stiff, stir 1 tbsp into mixture, then fold in remainder lightly. Turn into pastry case, and bake at 325°F, Gas 3, for 35–45 minutes until firm in the centre and lightly browned. Serve cold.

Cottage-orange cheesecake

2 eggs, separated
2 oz caster sugar
$\frac{3}{4}$ oz powdered gelatine
$\frac{1}{2}$ pint natural orange juice, fresh,
   frozen or canned
3 oz butter
8 oz crispbread crumbs
1 lb cottage cheese
1 orange

Put egg yolks, sugar, gelatine and juice in a metal basin and mix well. Stand basin in a container of very hot water and stir until gelatine dissolves. Put basin in a cool place and cool well. While cooling, cream butter until very soft. Mix with crumbs. Press mixture against sides and base of a 7 inch cake tin with removable base. Run a sharp knife round top of tin to remove loose crumbs. Chill case to firm up. Sieve cheese into a bowl, grate orange peel and stir it into cheese. As soon as juice mixture begins to set, stir in cheese lightly with a scooping movement. Whisk egg whites to same consistency and fold in. (If cheese mixture is already setting, stir in first tbsp.) Pour mixture gently into crumb shell, chill until set. Decorate with skinned orange segments.

(American: $1\frac{1}{4}$ cups juice)

Baked stuffed apples

Serves 4
4 medium cooking apples
4 oz cottage cheese
1 level teasp grated orange peel
1 oz sultanas (optional)
pinch of ground cloves
demerara sugar as needed
4 fl oz natural orange juice, fresh or
   canned
single cream or custard (optional)

Core apples without peeling. Slit skin of each round the middle without cutting deeply into flesh. Mix together cheese, peel, sultanas if used, spice and sugar to taste. Fill core holes in apples with mixture. Stand apples upright in a shallow baking tin. Pour orange juice over and top each apple with extra sugar. Bake 20–40 minutes at 350°F, Gas 4, until apples are tender but not mushy (time depends on type and size of apple). Serve hot, with single cream or custard if desired.

(American: 1¼ teasps peel and ½ cup juice, light cream)

caster sugar. Cut 8 slits in lid and open out well. Bake pie at 400°F, Gas 6, for 25–30 minutes or until golden brown. Cool slightly. Heat 3 fl oz cream to scalding (not boiling) and pour through slits into pie. Whip remaining cream and chill. Serve pie warm or cold with chilled whipped cream.

(American: 2–3 tbsps demerara sugar, ¾ cup heavy cream)

Blackstock pie

Serves 6–8
butter
10 oz short crust pastry
2 lb cooking apples (1½ lb prepared)
6 oz Cheddar cheese
1 egg white
2–3 dessertsps demerara sugar
6 fl oz double cream
caster sugar as needed

Grease an 8 inch pie dish and damp edge. Roll out slightly more than half pastry thinly, and line dish. Chill. Peel, core and slice apples thinly. Grate cheese. Beat egg white until liquid. Brush inside of pastry shell and rim with egg white. Pack in half apples, sprinkle with half the sugar and strew on half the cheese. Repeat these layers, using remaining fruit, sugar and cheese. Roll out remaining pastry and lay on top as lid. Press rim down firmly and flute. Brush with egg white, dredge with

Blackcurrant charlotte

Serves 6–8
24 sponge fingers
2 tbsps blackcurrant jam
8 oz fresh blackcurrants or 1 × 15 oz can blackcurrants
2 oz caster sugar if needed
8 oz cottage cheese, sieved
¼ pint soured cream
2 teasps powdered gelatine
2 tbsps fruit juice (from currants)
2 egg whites
whipped cream

Line a 1½ pint souffle dish with sponge fingers, sticking them together with jam. Cover base with fingers too. Simmer fresh fruit in a little water, with sugar, until soft and drain; if using canned fruit, drain and only sweeten to taste. Mix cheese into well drained fruit, and add soured cream. Dissolve gelatine in fruit juice over hot water, cool well and stir into cheese mixture. Whisk egg white stiffly. Fold into cheese mixture when on the point of setting. Chill until firm, then unmould. Decorate with whipped cream.

(American: 3 tbsps jam, 2½ teasps gelatine, 3 tbsps juice; use a 2 pint dish)

Candied orange cream

Serves 4–6
1½ oz ground almonds
1½ oz semolina
1½ oz candied orange peel, finely
    chopped
4 oz caster sugar
grated peel of 1 lemon
12 oz curd cheese, sieved
2 large egg yolks

Use whole candied orange peel, not chopped mixed peel. Mix together almonds, semolina, chopped peel, 3½ oz sugar and grated peel. Fold into sieved cheese. Beat egg yolks until liquid, and blend into mixture lightly but thoroughly. Pile mixture in serving dish, sprinkle with remaining ½ oz sugar and chill overnight. Serve with macaroons.

Raspberry fromage

Serves 2–3
8 oz frozen raspberries, thawed
4 oz cottage cheese, sieved
maraschino liqueur to taste (see
    recipe)
sugar to taste
sweetened single cream (optional)

Drain excess juice from fruit. Mix sieved cheese with about 2 teasps liqueur, either from a bottle of maraschino cherries or a miniature bottle. Add sugar to taste. Fork fruit lightly into cheese mixture, and chill for several hours. Just before serving, pour over a little of the excess raspberry juice, sweetened, if needed; the dessert should not be liquid but should have a little flowing juice with it. For a luxury, add a little single cream too. Serve in individual stemmed glasses, eg wine glasses.

Chocolate ice cream

Serves 4–5 per tray, 8–10 in all
2 × 3-oz pkts rich full-fat soft cheese
3½ oz caster sugar
8 fl oz milk
4 oz plain chocolate
8 fl oz double cream

Cream cheese and sugar together until smooth. Add milk gradually, beating continuously. Melt chocolate in a basin over hot water. Cool. When cooled but still very soft, beat in cheese mixture gradually until blended completely. Mix in cream likewise. Pour into 2 ice trays and freeze for 40–50 minutes or until needed. Serve in stemmed glasses.

Variations:
1. Place 1 tbsp crushed macaroon in

each serving glass, top with chopped fresh orange segments, cover with ice cream.

2. Place $\frac{1}{2}$ small chopped banana in each serving glass, cover with ice cream, decorate with chopped nuts.

(American: superfine sugar, 1 cup each milk and heavy cream)

Black cherry pastries

8 oz unsalted butter
4 oz caster sugar
2 hard-boiled egg yolks, sieved
1 egg yolk, raw
1 level teasp grated orange peel
2 teasps vanilla essence
$\frac{1}{2}$ teasp salt
8 oz flour
black cherry jam as needed
2 oz full-fat soft cheese
1 egg white
caster sugar

Cream butter and sugar until light and fluffy. Add sieved egg yolks, raw egg yolk, peel, essence, salt. Mix well. Add flour gradually; stir until a dough is obtained. Knead lightly, wrap in foil and chill 30 minutes. Roll out $\frac{1}{2}$ dough on floured surface to $\frac{1}{8}$th inch thick. Cut out 20 circles, $2\frac{1}{2}$ inches in diameter. Place on lightly greased baking sheets. Put a little cherry jam and cheese on each. Roll out remaining dough, cut out another 20 circles. Wet edges of jam-filled circles, press

on new circles as lids. Brush with beaten egg white, sprinkle with sugar. Bake at 350°F, Gas 4, for 10–15 minutes. Remove from sheets with spatula and cool on wire racks.

(American: extra flavourings, superfine sugar)

Gingerbread with cheese

6 tbsps milk
4 oz unsalted butter
4 oz soft brown sugar
6 oz black treacle
8 oz flour
good pinch each ground cloves, grated nutmeg, ground mace and coriander, 1 teasp in all
2 teasps ground ginger
1 level teasp each grated orange and lemon peel
2 teasps chopped candied peel
1 egg, beaten
1 level teasp bicarbonate of soda
thick slices Cheshire cheese to cover
   1×7 inch square cake

Melt butter, sugar, treacle and remaining milk in a pan without letting it get too hot. Stir while heating, then cool slightly off the heat. While cooling, sift flour and spices into a bowl, pour in egg. Dissolve soda in 1 warmed tbsp milk. Add the liquid ingredients. Mix thoroughly adding grated and candied peel.

Line a square 7 inch cake tin with greaseproof paper and brush with butter. Turn mixture into tin, smooth top if required; bake at 300°F, Gas 1–2, for about $1\frac{1}{4}$ hours. Cool 30 minutes in tin, then on wire rack. Store 2–3 days in airtight tin before use. To use, either serve with cheese; or split horizontally like sandwich cake, fill cheese between layers, keep a further 24 hours before use. Serve plain, or accompanied by preserved ginger or dessert apples.

(American: heaped $\frac{1}{2}$ teasp soda, $7\frac{1}{2}$–8 tbsps milk, extra ginger and peel to taste)

Fondues, souffles, rarebits and hearty savouries

The Swiss invented the cheese fondue, the British created rarebits or 'rabbits', the French made souffles known and Americans lay claim to the first toasted buns and sandwiches. All these are now traditional dishes. But we have developed many new variations as well. Fondues and souffles are usually full dinner or supper dishes, while 'rabbits' and toasted dishes make good tray suppers and snacks.

The essential thing to have for making a real Swiss fondue is the right kind of pan and spirit lamp. If the cheese cooks too quickly, even for a moment, the fondue becomes a ropey, sticky mass instead of a smooth, very thick sauce. It must be kept at an even, very low temperature; the opposite of a meat fondue, for which fat must be kept at high heat to sear the meat cubes instantly. The pans for these two fondues are entirely different. Besides the pan, all you need for serving a cheese fondue is crusty fresh bread cut in cubes, long-handled forks, and a plate and napkin for everyone.

Give each person a helping of bread cubes to dip in the sauce.

Today, there are very good fondue packet mixes on the market, and even the Swiss often use them.

Swiss cheese fondue

Cook this and all other fondues in a fondue pan on the kitchen stove and transfer the pan to the spirit lamp on the dining-room table when the fondue is ready.

12 oz Emmentaler cheese
12 oz Swiss Gruyere cheese
$\frac{1}{2}$ garlic clove
4 glasses white wine
3 teasps lemon juice
1 heaped teasp cornflour or potato flour
1 liqueur glass Kirsch
pepper or nutmeg

Shred cheeses. Rub inside of pan with cut side of garlic clove. Warm wine and juice in pan, add cheeses gradually, stirring with a whisk continuously. Mix flour and Kirsch to a smooth paste. Let cheese mixture boil up on moderate heat, then add the paste gradually, stirring to blend in. Season. Lower heat and continue cooking for a short time, stirring with figure 8 movements with whisk. When the fondue is thick and creamy, transfer the pan to the spirit lamp and serve at once.

Tea without milk is the traditional drink with fondue, although wine or beer can be served if preferred.

(American: $3\frac{1}{2}$ teasps juice, $2\frac{1}{2}$ level teasps cornstarch or flour)

English apple fondue

$\frac{1}{2}$ clove garlic
$\frac{3}{4}$ pint apple juice
1 level tbsp cornflour
$\frac{1}{4}$ level teasp dry mustard
$\frac{1}{4}$ level teasp paprika
$1\frac{1}{2}$ lb grated Cheddar cheese

Rub inside of heavy pan with cut side of garlic clove. Mix a little apple juice with the cornflour, mustard and paprika in a bowl. Warm remaining juice in pan, add cheese and stir until melted. Stir in cornflour mixture, raise heat and simmer gently 10–15 minutes until creamy, stirring continuously. Transfer pan to spirit lamp. Serve with cubes of apple tossed in lemon juice, or cubed toast.

(American: $1\frac{1}{4}$ tbsps cornstarch)

Cheese souffle

Serves 4
1 oz butter
1 oz flour
$\frac{1}{4}$ pint milk
3 eggs, separated
3 oz grated cheese
salt and pepper
pinch of Cayenne pepper

A souffle is light and airy because whisked egg whites are added. If it is knocked or left to stand, the hot air is jolted out or shrinks, and the souffle falls.

39

The classic way to cook a souffle is in a straight-sided ovenproof dish with a paper band tied round it, rising about 2 inches above the rim. The inside of dish and paper are greased. When the souffle is ready, the paper is peeled off so that the souffle is seen above the rim. A souffle can look just as good served in a deeper dish without the band. But the dish must still be greased inside.

Heat oven to 400°F, Gas 6. Melt the butter, stir in flour, and mix well. Stir in milk gradually, and bring to the boil while stirring. Cool slightly then add cheese. Mix in, then add egg yolks one at a time; mix in well and season. Whisk egg whites stiffly, fold in and turn mixture gently into prepared souffle dish. Bake for about 25 minutes until well risen and browned. Turn off oven, and leave souffle for 3–4 minutes to firm up. Remove carefully and serve at once.

(American: $\frac{1}{2}$ cup + 2 tbsps milk)

Welsh rabbit

Serves 4
slices of buttered toast
1 oz butter or margarine
1 tbsp flour
6 tbsps milk or 4 tbsps milk and
    2 tbsps ale or beer
1 teasp made English mustard
a few drops Worcester sauce

4–6 oz grated Cheddar cheese
salt and pepper

Make the toast before the rabbit mixture. Keep warm. To make the rabbit, heat the fat in a pan, stir in flour, cook together for a few moments, stirring continuously. Warm liquid, and add gradually to pan, still stirring. When mixture is very thick and smooth, add all other ingredients except toast. Stir to blend. As soon as cheese melts, remove from heat. Spread on toast and place under low grill to brown top. Serve at once.

For 1 or 2 servings, use only part of mixture. Cool the rest and store for another rabbit or as a topping for vegetables.

Variation: for Buck rabbit top each slice of rabbit with a poached egg.

(American: $1\frac{1}{4}$ tbsps flour, $7\frac{1}{2}$–8 tbsps milk, or 5 tbsps milk and $2\frac{1}{2}$ tbsps beer)

Victorian Welsh rare-bit

For each person use:
2 slices crustless white bread
butter
$\frac{1}{2}$ level teasp made English mustard
freshly ground black pepper
2 oz Cheshire cheese

Toast bread lightly both sides, butter one side. Lay buttered side up on a flameproof plate. Spread with mustard, sprinkle with pepper. Slice or flake cheese thinly and cover toast with it completely. Trim any overhanging bits. Cover loosely with sheet of foil. Place under very gentle grill to melt slowly. Serve as soon as cheese is soft and runny.

(American: extra mustard if desired)

Irish rabbit

Serves 2
2 large slices buttered toast without crusts
3 tbsps milk
1 oz margarine
4 oz grated Cheddar cheese
1 teasp vinegar
1 teasp made English mustard
salt and pepper
1 dessertsp chopped gherkin

Make toast and keep warm. Place milk, fat and cheese in a pan, stir over very gentle heat. As soon as cheese is melted and mixture is creamy, stir in vinegar, seasoning and gherkin. Pour mixture over toast, and brown top under grill if desired.

(American: 4 tbsps milk, $1\frac{1}{4}$ teasp each vinegar and mustard, 1 tbsp gherkin)

Cheese and egg toasts

Serves 2
4 slices French bread $\frac{1}{2}$ inch thick
4 oz Cheshire cheese
1 hard-boiled egg yolk
1 level dessertsp butter
extra butter for toast

Cut crusts off bread and trim with scissors or cut into neat rounds with a biscuit cutter. Grate cheese and crumble egg yolk. Soften butter slightly. Pound cheese, egg yolk and the dessertsp butter together to form a smooth paste. Toast bread lightly on both sides and butter one side. Spread buttered side thickly with cheese paste, covering completely. Place under grill for 2–3 minutes until surface bubbles and browns.

(American: American cheese, 1 tbsp butter)

Two-minute toasted puffs

Serves 2
4 slices white bread
2 spring onion bulbs, finely chopped
4 heaped tbsps stiff mayonnaise
4 heaped teasps grated Parmesan cheese

Cut 3 inch circles from bread, toast on one side. Leave grill lighted. Sprinkle untoasted bread side with onion, pile on mayonnaise to cover, top with cheese. Place under grill for 1–2 minutes to brown cheese. Serve quickly, piping hot.

(American: scallion for spring onion; 5 heaped tbsps mayonnaise, 5 heaped teasps Parmesan)

Blue cheese and apple slices

Serves 2 for supper or makes
    6 snacks
chilled parsley butter (see recipe)
3 oz blue cheese
1 oz butter or margarine
1 oz fine white breadcrumbs
2 large cooking apples
pepper
flour for dredging

Make parsley butter first: cream 2 oz
butter with 1 level teasp finely
chopped parsley and a few drops
lemon juice; season with salt and
pepper to taste. Form butter into
small balls and chill. Crumble the
cheese, and cream with fat. Mix in
breadcrumbs, and work to a stiff
paste. Core apples but do not peel
them. Cut each into 3 thick slices,
discarding the ends. Lay slices on a
baking sheet or foil plate. Season
with a very little pepper, and dredge
lightly with flour. Spread each with
cheese mixture all over. Grill under
gentle heat until cheese is bubbling
and brown on top. Leave in a warm
place for 2–3 minutes to soften apple.
Top each slice with a chilled parsley
butter ball just before serving.

Roasted cheese

Serves 4
1 egg yolk
1 oz softened butter
2 oz soft white breadcrumbs
1 level teasp dry English mustard
salt and pepper
1½ oz Cheshire cheese
4 slices white bread without crusts

Mix egg, then butter, with
breadcrumbs and seasoning. Grate
cheese, soften it with the back of a
spoon, add to breadcrumb mixture
and pound together until smooth.
Toast bread lightly on both sides,
spread one side of each slice thickly
with cheese paste. Place in shallow
heat or flameproof dish, cover loosely
with foil and heat either in the oven
or under a very gentle grill for 4–5
minutes until cheese is hot and some
of its fat has seeped into the toast.
Uncover to let mixture brown
slightly, raising heat if necessary.

(American: well aged full-fat
American cheese)

French cheese sandwiches

The French, who call these Croques
Monsieur, *have various ways of
making them. They are first class for
finishing up bread and butter and
scraps of cold cooked meat and cheese*

For each person, use:
2 slices crustless white bread, 3–4
    inches square
butter
thin slices or remnants of cooked
    ham or bacon to cover bread
thin slice of Gruyere cheese to
    cover bread

Butter bread. Make a sandwich with one thin layer meat and one of cheese. Trim edges. Lay on a well buttered foil plate and butter top of upper bread slice. Bake for about 10 minutes at 350°F, Gas 4, until golden. If you prefer, fry sandwich in butter on one side, then toast second side under grill.

Variation: substitute leftover luncheon meat for the ham or bacon if you wish.

Baked cheese sandwiches

This Victorian recipe makes a high tea dish or late night snack quite different from the usual toasted sandwiches.

For each person, use:
2 thin slices brown bread
butter
slice of Cheshire cheese, ½ inch thick
chopped parsley

Butter bread lightly and remove crusts. Place the slice of cheese between buttered sides to form a sandwich. Heat oven to 400°F, Gas 6, and bake sandwich for 7–10 minutes until top bread slice curls crisply at the corners, and cheese is soft but not melted. The sandwiches will be very hot so should be left for a moment or two before serving. But do not leave them long enough to let the cheese go ropey. Top with chopped parsley and eat with a knife and fork.

(American: well aged American cheese)

Baked cheese puddings

Serves 4–6
½ pint milk
2–3 oz white breadcrumbs
1½ oz grated Parmesan cheese
1½ oz grated Cheshire cheese
1 oz softened butter
2 eggs, separated
salt and pepper
pinch of ground mace

Butter 4–6 individual ramekins. Bring milk to boil in a pan, pour over breadcrumbs. Leave to stand 5–10 minutes. Stir to blend, then mix in cheeses and butter. Blend yolks well into cheese mixture. Season. Heat oven to 400°F, Gas 6. Whisk egg whites until stiff, fold into cheese mixture. If stiff, stir in 1 spoonful whites first. Turn mixture gently into buttered dishes. Bake 15–20 minutes until puddings are brown and crisp. Serve very hot.

(American: 1¼ cups milk)

Cheese omelette

Serves 2
4 eggs
2 tbsps milk
salt and pepper
pinch of grated nutmeg

4 oz finely grated cheese
unsalted butter, as needed

Whisk eggs with milk, seasonings and 2 oz cheese. Place a 6 inch omelette pan over gentle heat, and when hot, add enough butter to coat it. Pour half egg mixture into the hot fat. Stir with fork, drawing mixture from sides to centre, to let egg spill over at sides. Shake pan to prevent sticking. Just before all egg sets, sprinkle in $\frac{1}{2}$ oz cheese. Flip $\frac{1}{3}$ omelette over cheese, then fold over opposite $\frac{1}{3}$. Slide omelette on to a warmed plate, sprinkle with $\frac{1}{2}$ oz cheese. Make second omelette in the same way.

(American: $2\frac{1}{2}$–3 tbsps milk)

Cheddar and mushroom omelette

Serves 1–2
2 eggs
salt and pepper
1 tbsp water
1 oz Cheddar cheese
1 large mushroom
1 tbsp unsalted butter
good sprinkling grated Parmesan
    cheese

Place eggs, seasoning and water in bowl and whisk to blend. Grate Cheddar cheese and stir in. Chop mushroom finely. Melt butter in 6 inch omelette pan, add mushroom and saute gently until soft. Raise heat, tip in egg mixture and stir in mushroom with fork. Draw mixture from sides of pan to let liquid egg run underneath. When egg is semi-set, allow to cook 1–2 minutes to brown omelette underneath, and fold in half. Slide on to warmed plate, sprinkle with Parmesan. Serve at once.

(American: $1\frac{1}{4}$ tbsps water, $1\frac{1}{4}$ tbsps butter)

Eggs mornay

Serves 4
4 eggs
1 oz butter
1 oz flour
8 fl oz rich milk
2 fl oz white wine or cider
salt, pepper and grated nutmeg
2–3 oz grated Gouda cheese
1 dessertsp grated Gruyere cheese
4 slices dry toast

Boil eggs 10 minutes, then place in cold water for 2–3 minutes. Melt fat, add flour, cook together 2–4 minutes without colouring. Off the heat, add milk, then wine gradually, stirring well. Return to heat and stir until sauce thickens. Add seasoning and Gouda cheese mixed and stir until cheese melts. Shell eggs and halve lengthways. Place in shallow dish, coat with sauce, sprinkle with Gruyere cheese and brown briefly under moderate grill. Serve at once with triangles of toast.

(American: 1 cup milk, $\frac{1}{4}$ cup wine or cider, 1 tbsp Gruyere cheese)

Eggs in moonlight

Serves 4
1$\frac{1}{4}$ lb mashed potato (1 × 4$\frac{1}{2}$ oz packet instant potato)
melted butter
5 eggs
1 oz Danish Blue cheese, crumbled
3 oz grated Samsoe or other firm mild cheese

Beat the potato well with 1 egg. Grease an ovenproof serving dish with melted butter and spread the potato over the base in a layer about 1 inch thick. Brush with a little more butter and make 4 dents in the surface to hold 4 poached eggs. Reheat in the oven at 375°F, Gas 5, until very hot. Meanwhile, poach the remaining eggs in salted water, stock or an egg poacher with butter-lined cups. Mix the cheeses together. When the eggs are poached, slide them into the spaces made in the hot potato, cover with the cheese and reheat if required until the cheese begins to melt. Serve at once.

(American: Fontina cheese for Samsoe)

Cheese fritters or beignets

Serves 2–4
8 fl oz water
4 oz butter
4 oz flour
1 teasp salt
4 eggs
5 oz grated Swiss Gruyere cheese
1$\frac{1}{2}$ tbsps cornflour
oil or fat for deep frying
a little finely grated Swiss Gruyere cheese to garnish

Heat water to boiling point, tip in butter, flour and salt and stir quickly until it forms a ball. Add eggs, one at a time, beating each in before adding the next. Stir until batter leaves sides of pan clean. Add cheese and cornflour mixed, blend in thoroughly. Leave to stand 3 hours. Heat oil or fat, drop in teaspoonfuls of batter, a few at a time. They should swell, turn and pop in the fat until full size and golden brown. Drain well on soft kitchen paper, keep warm until all fritters are fried. Sprinkle with extra cheese and serve at once.

(American: 1 cup water, $\frac{1}{2}$ cup butter, 1 cup flour, 1$\frac{1}{4}$ teasps salt, 2 tbsps cornstarch)

Georgian croquets

About 12 croquets
1 oz fine soft white breadcrumbs
1 oz finely grated Cheddar cheese

pinch each salt and pepper
pinch of Cayenne pepper
2 egg whites
fat for deep frying
1 tbsp grated Parmesan cheese

Mix the breadcrumbs and Cheddar cheese in a bowl and add seasonings. Beat the egg whites until they just hold peaks but are still moist. Fold into the breadcrumb-cheese mixture. Form lightly into balls the size of a walnut. Heat deep oil or fat to 375°F, Gas 5 (hot enough to brown a bread cube in 30 seconds). Fry the cheese balls until golden brown. Serve sprinkled with Parmesan.

(American: 1½ tbsps Parmesan)

Baked goods, sandwiches and spreads

The baked goods in this section include scones and sandwiches, pizzas, savoury pastries and biscuits. There are suggestions, too, for a variety of sandwich shapes and fillings, for family use and parties.

Sandwiches are useful standbys for a family or crowd. Try different kinds: decker, pinwheel, rolled or pyramid. Or try open or toasted sandwiches (see recipes). Vary them by using different breads: white, brown, wholewheat, malt, rye and fruit breads are all good with cheeses.

For fried sandwiches, make ordinary sandwiches with non-run fillings, dip them in egg and milk quickly, drain and fry in a little butter.

Any of the potted cheeses recipes in this section makes a good cold spread or filling for sandwiches, vols-au-vent, canapes and so on. The value of potted cheeses is that you can make them at any convenient moment, using up leftovers. One or two can be kept ready as a standby for family use, or several can be made in advance for a party. They will wait patiently in the refrigerator for up to a week without coming to harm.

Cheese bread

8 oz self-raising flour
1 level teasp dry mustard
1 level teasp salt
pinch of pepper
3 oz margarine
4 oz Farmhouse Cheddar cheese
2 eggs
$\frac{1}{4}$ pint milk

Sieve flour and seasonings, and rub in fat. Grate cheese, and stir in. Beat eggs and milk together and mix into dry ingredients, to a soft dropping consistency. Place mixture in a greased 1-lb loaf tin, smooth top with hot wet knife, and bake at 350°F, Gas 4, for $\frac{3}{4}$–1 hour until cooked through. Cool on a wire tray.

(American: 2 cups flour, extra seasoning if desired, $\frac{1}{2}$ cup + 2 tbsps milk)

Cheese scones

6 scones
8 oz self-raising flour
pinch each salt and dry mustard
1 oz butter
2 oz grated Cheddar cheese
milk to mix

Sift flour, salt and mustard into a bowl. Rub in butter. Add almost all the cheese. Mix with milk to a soft dough. Turn on to a floured surface, and pat into a round about $\frac{1}{2}$ inch thick. Cut in half, then cut each half into 3 triangles. Brush with milk and sprinkle with remaining cheese. Place on a baking sheet. Bake at 425°F, Gas 7, for 8–10 minutes. Serve hot or cold, split and buttered if liked.

Cheese scone ring

2 oz butter
8 oz self-raising flour
pinch of salt
4 oz mild grated cheese (Esrom or Samsoe)
1 level teasp dried basil

Rub butter into flour until like fine crumbs. Add salt and milk to make a firm dough. Knead, then roll out to oblong about 13 × 9 inches in size. Spread cheese all over dough, scatter herbs on top. Roll up pastry like a swiss roll, and cut into 8 slices. Grease a baking sheet. Arrange pastry slices in a circle, touching each other, on sheet. Bake at 425°F, Gas 7, for 15–20 minutes until golden. Cool on the sheet. Serve with Cream and parsley dip (see p 57).

(American: use extra herbs if desired)

Pizza

Serves 4–6
$\frac{1}{4}$ pint milk
1 teasp sugar
$\frac{1}{4}$ oz dried yeast
8 oz strong plain flour

1 level teasp salt
2 oz margarine
1 egg, beaten
1 lb tomatoes, skinned and sliced
$\frac{1}{2}$ oz minced onion
1 level tbsp dried basil
$\frac{1}{4}$ minced garlic clove (optional)
2 tbsps olive oil
3 oz grated mild cheese (Bel Paese,
    Gouda or Port Salut)
2 oz stoned black olives
1×2 oz can anchovy fillets, drained

Warm milk to blood heat. Dissolve sugar in milk, sprinkle on the yeast and leave in a warm place until frothy. Mix flour and salt, rub in fat, stir in yeast liquid and milk, and egg. Make a fairly soft dough. Knead for about 10 minutes, then cover and leave to rise. Meanwhile, fry tomatoes, onions and herbs gently in oil for 5 minutes without browning. Drain.

When dough has doubled in size, knead lightly, place in greased 8 inch cake tin, press out to cover base and top with tomato mixture. Scatter cheese over. Arrange olives and anchovy fillets in a lattice pattern on top. Leave to prove about 15 minutes. Brush with oil, and bake at 400°F, Gas 6, for about 30 minutes.

Variations: for Tomato-Cheddar pizza use 3 oz thinly sliced mild Cheddar cheese; for Emmentaler-gherkin pizza use 3 oz thinly sliced Emmentaler cheese, substitute chopped gherkin pieces for olives.

(American: $\frac{1}{2}$ cup + 2 tbsps milk, $1\frac{1}{4}$ teasps sugar, salt to taste, $1\frac{1}{4}$ tbsps basil, $2\frac{1}{2}$ tbsps oil)

Quick kipper pizza

Serves 4–6
8 oz self-raising flour
1 teasp salt
$1\frac{1}{2}$ oz butter
$\frac{1}{4}$ pint milk, approx
4 oz grated Cheddar cheese
1 teasp dry mustard
1 teasp dried mixed herbs
$\frac{1}{2}$ lb tomatoes
8 stoned black olives
8 kipper fillets
paprika

Sift flour and salt together, rub in fat until like crumbs. Bind with enough milk to make soft dough. Roll out into 12 inch circle and place on greased baking sheet. Chill. Mix grated cheese, mustard and herbs in a bowl. Sprinkle over dough. Arrange thinly sliced tomatoes on top, then place kipper fillets like wheel spokes on tomatoes. Put olives between fillets. Sprinkle with paprika. Bake at 400°F, Gas 6, for about 30 minutes.

(American: extra salt, mustard and herbs to taste)

Cheese pastry

4 oz plain flour
pinch of salt and white pepper
1 oz margarine
1 oz lard
2 oz finely grated Cheddar cheese
water to mix

Mix flour, salt and pepper, and rub in fat until mixture is like crumbs. Mix in cheese. Stir in water until mixture begins to form lumps. Knead by hand to smooth dough. Roll out, chill and use like short crust pastry. Bake with a savoury filling at 400°F, Gas 6. Dough made with 4 oz flour rolled ⅛th inch thick should line a 7–8 inch pie plate or flan ring.

To bake blind, wholly or partly: preheat oven. Line pastry base with greaseproof paper and dried beans. Bake for 8–9 minutes until pastry edges shrink slightly. Remove paper and beans. Bake a further 7–10 minutes for a fully baked shell, 2–3 minutes only for a partly baked one.

(American: 1 cup all-purpose flour)

Victorian cheese straws

4–5 dozen straws
4 oz butter
4 oz flour
4 oz white bread without crusts
4 oz Gouda cheese
pinch each salt and Cayenne pepper

Soften the butter and sift the flour. Grate bread and cheese together. Mix all ingredients with a fork into a crumbly mass, then work with the hands into a smooth dough. Chill for at least 30 minutes. Heat oven to 350°F, Gas 4. Roll out dough ¼ inch thick on a well floured surface. Cut into thin straws ⅛th inch wide and about 2 inches long (like straw potatoes). Bake for 10–12 minutes.

(American: ½ cup butter, 1 cup flour, a good pinch of each seasoning)

Cheese shortbread fingers

About 3 dozen fingers
4 oz butter
4 oz flour
4 oz grated Edam or Gouda cheese
¼ teasp each salt and Cayenne pepper

Soften the butter and sift the flour. Mix together, using a rotary or electric mixer if possible. Mix in cheese and seasonings. The dough will be soft, even sticky. Form into a ball, divide in half and chill both portions at least 30 minutes. When ready to bake, heat oven to 350°F, Gas 4. Prepare one portion of dough, leaving second chilled. Roll out dough on well floured surface to ¼ inch thickness. Cut in fingers 3–4 inches long and about ⅓ inch wide. Bake for 15–17 minutes. Deal with second portion of dough like the first.

(American: $\frac{1}{2}$ cup butter, 1 cup flour, extra seasoning if required)

Cheese sandwiches

Quantities of butter and fillings will vary, but for a party allow an average of $\frac{3}{4}$ lb butter for 50 slices bread and 3 lb for 200 slices.

Decker sandwiches
Use 3 or 4 slices white or brown bread with 2 or 3 fillings for each. For striped deckers, alternate white and brown slices or use differently coloured, gay fillings.

Pinwheel sandwiches
For each sandwich use 1 thin soft white and 1 thin soft brown slice bread, cut lengthways from loaf. Spread filling thinly and roll up like a Swiss roll. Cut the roll into thin slices.

Rolled sandwiches
As pinwheel sandwiches but using 1 bread slice only, brown or white as preferred. Dark rye bread makes unusual rolled sandwiches.

Pyramid sandwiches
Cut 5 different sizes of bread circles varying in diameter from 1 to 4 inches. Butter, spread and stack with smallest at top. Vary colours and flavours of spreads.

Cheese sandwich fillings or spreads

Season cheese well with salt and pepper or sugar as appropriate. Use additional ingredients below as available, or to taste. (See also potted cheeses, pp 53-54).
Note: for toasted and fried sandwiches, avoid soft and fatty cheeses, buttery or oily mixtures, jams, nuts, syrups and strongly flavoured additions such as olives.

Full fat soft cheese with:
chutney
chopped soaked figs or prunes
canned salmon or crab with a little
  lemon juice
minced ham and (optional) cucumber
finely chopped eating apple, chopped
  fresh mint and lemon juice
crushed well drained pineapple and
  preserved ginger
crushed strawberries or raspberries,
  sugar and lemon juice

Cottage cheese with:
minced spring onion and scrambled
  egg
sieved hard-boiled egg yolk and
  mayonnaise
minced cooked bacon, ham or
  luncheon meat
grated onion and caraway seeds
mashed liver or game pate
flaked tuna fish and lemon juice
chopped or mashed sardines and
  lemon juice
finely chopped pineapple and raisins

51

Cheddar cheese *grated:*
mixed with sour cream and
   minced smoked haddock or cod
grated, mixed to a paste with hard-
   boiled egg yolks and anchovy
   essence or paste
grated, mashed to a paste with
   mayonnaise and minced capers
flaked, with sliced cucumber
flaked, with sliced tomato
sliced, topped with ½ bacon rasher
sliced, with chutney
sliced, with tomato puree and a few
   drops Tabasco
sliced, spread with French or English
   mustard and tomato sauce
sliced, topped with chopped lightly
   cooked mushrooms

Cheshire cheese, *crumbled*, with:
shredded apple and curd cheese
mashed cooked pear
minced spring onion and cream
scrambled egg and chopped parsley
flaked with:
tomato slices and chopped fresh
   mint

Edam or Gouda cheese, *sliced,*
spread with:
mashed herring fillet
thinly sliced tomato and black pepper
sliced dill pickles or cocktail gherkins
chopped stoned olives and
   mayonnaise
grated sharp apple and a light
   sprinkling curry powder
minced watercress and a little sour
   cream

Gruyere or Emmentaler cheese,
grated, with:
grated apple and curd cheese
Parmesan cheese and butter mashed
   to a paste

Esrom or Samsoe cheese, *sliced,*
spread with:
chutney
sliced smoked sausage
shredded cooked bacon
shredded lettuce and chopped
   peanuts

Danish Blue cheese, *crumbled*, with:
cottage or curd cheese
cucumber slices and chopped walnuts
soft cooked rice and grated apple
butter and a little brandy

Open sandwiches

Use one thick slice brown or rye
bread or ½ split soft round roll.
Make toppings colourful and
decorative.

1. Cover brown bread with lettuce
leaf, top with flaked Cheddar cheese
and sliced apple. Decorate with
mayonnaise, chopped parsley.

2. Cover brown bread with mustard-
flavoured butter, then lettuce leaf
and sliced Esrom or Samsoe cheese.
Arrange sliced liver sausage on top,
decorate with crumbled hard-boiled
egg.

3. Cover brown bread with sliced
Esrom or Samsoe cheese. Arrange

4–5 orange or mandarin sections and halved cucumber slices on top in decorative pattern. Sprinkle with chopped parsley.

4. Arrange thin slices Danish Blue cheese on bread, pipe border of full fat soft cheese around it. Stud border with baby coloured cocktail onions at intervals.

5. Cover bread with slice of ham, then sliced Gouda or Edam cheese. Lay 2 asparagus spears diagonally across bread slice, hold in place with piped rosettes of soft cheese.

6. Spread bread with Brie cheese instead of butter, decorate with alternate diagonal bands of crumbled hard-boiled egg yolk and finely chopped parsley.

Toasted sandwiches

Toast ordinary closed sandwiches under grill, using non-run fillings.

For **toasted decker sandwiches,** toast closed decker sandwiches firmly pressed together, as above.

For **toasted rolled sandwiches,** brush rolled sandwiches with melted butter, grill on each side briefly till brown.

For **quick toasted sandwiches,** make sandwiches with 2 pieces hot toast.

For **toasted club sandwiches,** make deckers with 3 slices hot toast; use thick fillings, spear sandwiches with cocktail sticks to hold them together.

For **super club sandwiches,** make club sandwiches as above and cover with cheese sauce (see p 9). Brown briefly under grill.

Potted Cheddar with walnuts

8 oz grated Cheddar cheese
3 oz unsalted butter, softened
1 mustardsp made English mustard
pinch of chilli powder
1 tbsp mild vinegar
12 chopped walnuts
clarified butter

Mix cheese and butter. Mix mustard with vinegar. Crush walnuts almost as fine as crumbs. Blend all ingredients well. Press down into small pots leaving $\frac{1}{2}$ inch headspace, tapping on the table to knock out air bubbles while filling. Cover with melted clarified butter if not for immediate use. Use as a spread or, mixed with breadcrumbs, as a stuffing for tomatoes served with a salad.

(American: $\frac{1}{8}$ teasp mustard, 4 teasps vinegar)

Potted cheese with sherry

4 oz unsalted butter
1 lb Cheddar or Cheshire cheese
salt
ground mace
medium sweet or cream sherry
melted clarified butter

Soften butter and grate cheese.
Pound about $\frac{1}{3}$ cheese with butter
until smooth (or process in electric
blender). Add rest of cheese with
spice and sherry to taste, and pound
or blend to a smooth paste. Press into
pots, tapping to knock out air holes
while filling. Leave $\frac{1}{2}$ inch headspace
and cover with clarified butter. Use
as a sandwich spread or filling for
choux.

Potted Stilton

$\frac{1}{2}$ lb butter
2 lb Stilton
salt
powdered mace
port
clarified butter

Pound butter and cheese in a mortar.
Season with salt and mace, moisten
with a very little port and press down
well in little pots. Cover with
clarified butter.

Cheese butter

2 oz unsalted butter
4 oz grated Cheddar cheese

1 tbsp milk
salt and pepper
$\frac{1}{4}$ teasp made English mustard

Place all ingredients in the top of a
double saucepan over simmering
water. Stir until cheese is melted and
blended in. Turn into small pots.
When cold, cover with greaseproof
paper or a lid. Use as a spread. Keeps
about a week.

(American: use extra mustard if
desired)

Crowdie butter

*This makes a good spread or filling
for a savoury sandwich loaf*

4 oz unsalted butter
8 oz Highland Crowdie low fat soft
    cheese
onion or garlic salt to taste

Soften butter. Mix all the ingredients,
and beat until thoroughly blended.
Chill before using.

(American: use any unsalted,
smooth low fat soft cheese)

Cheese for parties

Use the dips at the beginning of this section for a small party or just for the family. Serve them with small salted crackers, fingers of toast, pumpernickel or potato crisps. You can also provide a selection of 3 inch pieces of celery, scraped young carrots, quartered lengthways, raw cauliflower sprigs and 3 inch pieces of quartered cucumber as 'dunkers' Add a little milk to any of the dips you want more liquid.

To serve a crowd, see pp 58–62. The quantities given should only be treated as a guide, especially for the gateaux, since much depends on the type of party, the other food being offered, and on whether the guests are hungry.

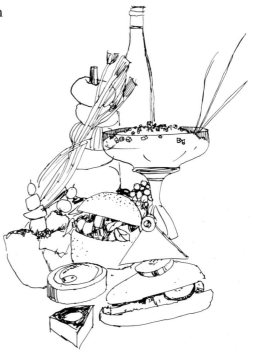

At the end of this section you will find ideas for a special cheese buffet or cheese tasting party. A cheese buffet or cheese tasting party makes an interesting change from ordinary supper food, especially if any guests do not eat meat or fish.

Serve a handsome cheese buffet to a crowd, either as a full supper or as part of a wine and cheese or cheese and ale party. You will find you can surprise people pleasantly by the variety of cheeses you can offer. Little work is involved, too, since you only have to buy and unwrap the cheeses, butter and breads and give each guest a knife and one plate.

Keep numbers down to between twelve and sixteen if you want people to taste and compare the cheeses properly. In this case, choose your cheeses carefully. Serve, for instance, both Farmhouse English and creamery Cheddar and Lancashire, and unwrapped and prepackaged Stilton, and ask guests to compare the two kinds; or contrast Danish, Dutch and French cheeses of a similar type. Try other variations too, including soft and processed cheeses. Use your own ideas to vary the cheeses suggested below.

There is no hard and fast rule about the type of drink to serve with cheese. Certainly wines are delicious; but now that wine and cheese parties are so well known, you may prefer to try an alternative.

If you serve wines, remember that a full flavoured white wine such as an Alsatian Riesling goes well with milder cheeses, while red wines suit the stronger cheeses better. Keep the heavier and fortified wines for strong, full cheeses such as blue cheeses; acid cheeses need the dryer, lighter red wines.

A choice of ciders, from dry to sweet, makes one of the best, time-honoured alternatives to wines. Offer at least one still cider; and try to include one of the excellent ciders made by smaller firms. Some of the drier types are subtle, exciting drinks.

Beers and ales, from light lagers to stout, are another good choice. Again, marry the lighter beers to the milder cheeses; German and Dutch lagers go well with semi-soft cheeses, for instance.

Cheddar dip

2 oz softened butter
8 oz grated Cheddar cheese
4 oz chopped ham
½ pint milk
1 teasp tomato puree
1 teasp salad cream
pinch of salt
pinch of Cayenne pepper

Cream butter well and mix in cheese and ham. Stir in milk gradually, add puree, salad cream and seasonings, and mix well. Pile on a dish, and lay dippers round pile.

(American: $1\frac{1}{4}$ cups milk, $1\frac{1}{4}$ teasps tomato puree, extra salad cream if desired)

Cream and parsley dip

4 fl oz soured cream
2 oz sieved cottage cheese
2 rashers crisply fried bacon, crumbled, 1 oz each
salt and black pepper to taste
pinch of curry powder
2–3 teasps chopped parsley

Combine all ingredients, and mix well. Add a little milk if a more liquid dip is desired.

Blue cheese dip

4 oz any blue cheese
2 tbsps mayonnaise
2 tbsps finely chopped green pepper
6 fl oz soured cream

Crumble the cheese into a bowl and lightly mash it with a fork. Stir in the mayonnaise and then the soured cream until the mixture is smooth. Lastly add the finely chopped green pepper. Pile the dip into a shallow bowl and serve chilled with biscuits.

(American: 3 tbsps mayonnaise, 3 tbsps chopped pepper and $\frac{3}{4}$ cup soured cream)

Ham and onion dip

2×3 oz pkts rich full fat soft cheese
1 dessertsp finely chopped spring onion green
1 dessertsp milk
pinch of salt
2 oz chopped ham

Cream the cheese in a bowl until soft. Mix in all the other ingredients. Add extra milk if you want a more liquid dip.

(American: use 1 tbsp each green onion and milk)

Creamy Camembert dip

1×8 oz ripe Camembert cheese
1×3 oz pkt rich full fat soft cheese
2 tbsps milk
4 full tbsps double cream
freshly ground pepper

Scrape or cut rind off Camembert. Chop coarsely with soft cheese and milk. Rub through sieve or pound until smooth. Add cream, season to taste, and mix until completely smooth and blended. Add more cream if needed to give consistency desired.

(American: $2\frac{1}{2}$ tbsps milk, 5 tbsps heavy cream)

Party croutes

	For 12	25
Bread slices	48	100
Butter		
for toasted croutes	8 oz	1 lb
for fried croutes		
For fried croutes		
Eggs, beaten	3	6
Breadcrumbs, fresh or dried	4 oz	8–10 oz
Oil for deep frying		

Toasted croutes
Cut a 2 inch circle from the centre of each bread slice. Toast lightly on both sides. Butter toast, cover with filling (see below) and decorate to taste (see Open sandwiches, pp 52–53).

Fried croutes
Cut a 2 inch circle from each bread slice. Butter one side of each. Sandwich in pairs with non-run filling. Dip in egg, coat firmly with crumbs. Deep fry in oil for 3 4 minutes, turning to brown second side if required. Drain well, cool, wrap in foil until required. Reheat briefly in oven to crisp.

Fillings

	For 12	25
1. grated Cheddar cheese	6 oz	12 oz
apples, peeled, cored and chopped	8 oz	1 lb
onion, finely chopped	2 oz	4 oz
dried mixed herbs	$\frac{1}{2}$ teasp	1 teasp
salt and pepper to taste		

Mix all ingredients thoroughly, mashing out lumps with a fork.

	For 12	25
2. onions, finely chopped	2 oz	4 oz
margarine	1 oz	2 oz
tomatoes, canned	12 oz	$1\frac{1}{2}$ lb
cornflour	$\frac{1}{2}$ tbsp	1 tbsp
dried basil	$\frac{1}{2}$ teasp	1 teasp
salt and pepper to taste		
grated Cheddar cheese	6 oz	12 oz

Fry onions in fat gently for 5 minutes. Add tomatoes and simmer for 15 minutes. Season. Mix cornflour with water, stir in. Cook 2 minutes. Remove from heat, cool slightly, stir in cheese. In America, use heaped spoons of cornstarch and herbs.

Savoury party gateau

$1 \times 7\frac{1}{2}$ oz pkt frozen short crust
    pastry
18–24 slices white bread
    ($1 \times 1\frac{3}{4}$ lb tin loaf)
$\frac{3}{4}$ lb butter, softened
For decoration: thinly sliced
    radishes or cucumber

Fillings

use 3 oz of the butter with each of the following:

1. 4 crumbled hard-boiled egg yolks
   1 tbsp double cream
   salt and pepper to taste
   a few drops yellow food colouring
   1 oz finely grated Cheddar cheese
2. 1×4 oz pkt frozen chopped
    spinach, thawed and drained
   1 oz cottage cheese, sieved
   2–3 spring onion bulbs
   salt as needed
   freshly ground black pepper to
    taste
   grated nutmeg to taste
3. 1×7 oz can herrings in tomato
    sauce

Icing

1 lb cottage cheese, sieved
$\frac{1}{4}$ pint double cream
$\frac{1}{2}$ oz gelatine
salt and pepper to taste

Use a 9 inch round cake tin. Turn it upside down and cover with oiled greaseproof paper or silicone treated parchment. Roll out the pastry $\frac{1}{8}$ inch thick and cover bottom of tin with a 9 inch circle of pastry. Bake blind at 375°F, Gas 5, for 6–7 minutes or until pastry is cooked and beginning to crisp. Cool completely. While cooling, cut crusts off bread slices and prepare fillings:

1. Work butter and egg yolks to a smooth paste. Add remaining ingredients gradually and beat or process in electric blender until smooth.

2. Squeeze any remaining liquid from spinach. Add butter and cheese and blend in thoroughly. Chop onion finely and mix in with flavourings.

3. Pick out any bones from fish. Beat fish and sauce with butter until well blended.

Assemble gateau. Cut bread slices diagonally, into triangles. Slide pastry circle on to a flat plate or tray. Spread thinly with butter. Cover with 1 layer bread; use part of 1 triangle, cut in pieces, to fill centre. Trim edges of bread to shape of pastry with sharp knife or scissors. Cover bread thinly with butter, then cover evenly with the fish filling. Repeat layers of bread, butter and fillings, using spinach filling first, then egg filling. Top with final layer of bread, but do not butter it. Chill gateau while making 'icing'.

Beat cheese and cream together until smooth. Soften gelatine in 2 tbsps water, then place container in small pan of very hot water and stir until gelatine dissolves. Beat into cheese and cream mixture at once. Chill briefly until beginning to thicken. Pour over top of gateau. Chill again until nearly firm. With warm wet knife, smooth on sides of gateau, to cover. (Store any remaining 'icing' for use as spread or dip.) Chill gateau until required, then decorate with sliced radishes or cucumber as preferred.

(American: 1¼ tbsps heavy cream for filling, 2½ tbsps water for softening gelatine, ½ cup plus 2 tbsps for 'icing')

Four-in-one cheese

It saves time, work and money to buy one large piece of cheese for a party instead of small quantities of different ones. One round, red 4 lb Edam cheese gives 4 exciting party variations, so that you need no other.

Cut about ⅓ off one end of the cheese. Take care to cut straight through so that the 2 pieces stand level when cut sides are undermost. Cut 2 flat circles of cheese about ¾ inch thick from the cut end of the bigger piece of cheese. You should now have 4 pieces of cheese: 2 flat circles, and 2 bowl shapes from the 2 ends. Scoop out the insides of the 2 bowl shapes, leaving each with about a ½ inch shell. Shred the 2 piles of scooped-out cheese separately. Now make the 4 cheese buffet dishes. Serve them with any 'dunker' or with toasted croutes (see p 58).

Circus cheese

shredded cheese from one 'bowl'
6 fl oz natural yogurt
1 × 4 oz bottle pimento stuffed olives, drained and chopped
1 medium onion
¼ pint beer

Make triangular cuts all round the edge of 1 cheese 'bowl'. Reserve these. Mix together the shredded cheese, yogurt and olives. Grate in ¾ of the onion. Mix well, using a rotary or electric mixer if possible. Add enough beer while mixing, to make a stiff paste. Fill the 'bowl' with mixture, using a fork to give a rough surface. (Not all the mixture will be needed.) Decorate top of mixture with reserved cheese triangles, red side uppermost.

Add any remaining beer to rest of mixture to make a dip. Serve separately.

Mountain cheese

1 tbsp sesame seeds
shredded cheese from 2nd 'bowl'
6 fl oz natural yogurt
2 teasps French mustard
2 tbsps Dutch Jenever or London gin
2 tbsps cottage cheese
5–6 sprigs parsley

Toast seeds in the oven at 350°F,
Gas 4, for 5 minutes or until golden.
Cool. Blend shredded cheese and
yogurt. Mix in mustard, Jenever or
gin and seeds, using rotary or electric
mixer if possible. Pile mixture high
into 2nd bowl and roughen surface
with a fork. Decorate with cottage
cheese to resemble snow. Place
parsley sprigs round base of pile as
'trees'.

(American: 2½ teasps mustard,
1 extra teasp Jenever or gin, also
sesame seeds, 3 tbsps cottage cheese)

Cheese and grape basket

2 small bunches black grapes
narrow coloured ribbon
Wash grapes. Place 1 bunch in the
centre of 1 cheese circle. Separate
grapes of 2nd bunch. Spear on
cocktail picks. Stick picks upright
into edge of cheese circle all round,
like the staves of a wicker basket. Tie
with ribbon. Serve circle on flat
platter with red edge showing.
Provide knife for cutting wedges or
cubes.

Cheese fish tank

1 × 7 oz can sardines, drained
1 × 4 oz can prawns or shrimps,
   drained
salt and pepper
½ small cucumber, diced
1 × 10 oz can condensed cream of
   celery soup
2 fl oz double cream, whipped

Cut a round hole in the centre of 2nd
cheese circle, leaving a rim about
1½ inch wide. Season cucumber, and
half fill hole with dice to represent
water. Lay sardines and prawns in
decorative pattern on the cucumber.
Serve with knife for cutting cheese
cubes and small forks for fish. Shred
cheese taken from hole, and mix with
soup from can. Fold in whipped
cream lightly, season to taste. Serve
as dip with the cheese fish tank or
separately with dunkers (see p 55).

Cheese buffet for twelve

12 oz Camembert
1¼ lb Brie
12 oz Gouda, Havarti or Samsoe
1 lb Cheddar or Cheshire
12 oz Wensleydale
12 oz Stilton or Mycella
3 bunches radishes
8 oz nuts and raisins
3–4 small bunches black grapes
1 large cucumber
2 heads salad celery
1 lb butter
French bread, crispbread, wholemeal
   or rye bread, assorted crackers
French mustard

Unwrap cheeses and leave at room temperature for 1–2 hours. Prepare salad ingredients and fruit. Top and tail radishes, wash grapes, cut cucumber in 2½ inch sticks and quarter lengthways, scrape and cut stem ends off celery. Cut cheeses in half or into three and arrange on cardboard platters. Arrange saladings and cheeses in 3 or 4 groups on a long table, with a tray of breads and biscuits between each group so that everyone can reach them easily. Serve with a choice of ciders, light red wines or beers.

Cheese and fruit buffet for six

Using fresh fruit is one of the most attractive ways to decorate a buffet meal of plain bread and cheese; and it provides a ready made dessert.

10–12 oz Camembert
16–18 oz mild Cheddar
8–10 oz Double Gloucester or Red
    Leicester
8–10 oz Caerphilly
8 oz Stilton
watercress
green and red sweet peppers
cucumber
black grapes
mandarin segments
red cherries
cooked prunes
skinned apricot halves
cottage cheese
breads and biscuits of your choice
butter
French mustard
mango chutney

Unwrap cheeses and leave at room temperature for 1–2 hours. Wash and trim cress, slice pepper across in thin circles, cube cucumber, salt it and leave for 1 hour to drain on a plate. Wash grapes, take pith off mandarin segments, wash cherries and stone prunes. Stuff prunes with cottage cheese. Arrange the cheeses at intervals around a circular table, keeping aside about ⅓ of the Cheddar. Cube this and spear on to cocktail sticks with the drained cucumber. Arrange with the other cheeses. Decorate Camembert with watercress, block of Cheddar with peppers, Gloucester or Leicester with grapes, Caerphilly with mandarin segments, and Stilton with cherries. Arrange the cheese and cucumber kebabs on a platter with the prunes and apricots; they will make a dramatic colour contrast. Arrange plates of bread or biscuits at intervals around the table behind the cheeses so that they are easily reached. Serve with white or rosé wines.

Index